# LINDBERGH ALONE

## ALONE

May 21, 1927

Other books by **Brendan Gill**

Death in April
The Trouble of One House
The Day the Money Stopped
Cole
Tallulah
Happy Times
Ways of Loving
Here at The New Yorker

# LINDBERGH ALONE

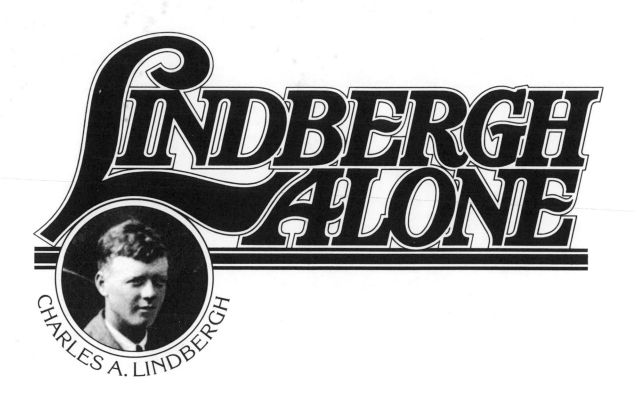

CHARLES A. LINDBERGH

By
## BRENDAN GILL

Harcourt Brace Jovanovich
New York and London

Printed in the United States of America.

Grateful acknowledgment is made to the following for permission to reprint material: Charles Scribner's Sons for quotations from The Spirit of St. Louis by Charles A. Lindbergh, copyright 1953 by Charles Scribner's Sons; Doubleday & Company, Inc., from The Hero by Kenneth S. Davis, copyright © 1959 by Kenneth S. Davis; G. P. Putnam's Sons, from We: His Own Story by Charles A. Lindbergh, copyright 1927, renewed 1955, by Charles A. Lindbergh; Harcourt Brace Jovanovich, Inc., from "Autobiography of Values" by Charles A. Lindbergh, copyright © 1977 by Harcourt Brace Jovanovich, Inc. and Anne Morrow Lindbergh, and The Wartime Journals of Charles A. Lindbergh, copyright © 1970 by Charles A. Lindbergh; Minnesota Historical Society, from Boyhood on the Upper Mississippi: A Reminiscent Letter by Charles A. Lindbergh, copyright © 1972 by The Minnesota Historical Society; The Charles A. Lindbergh Papers, Yale University Library and Anne Morrow Lindbergh, from Charles A. Lindbergh's diary and letters and from letters of Charles A. Lindbergh, Sr. and Evangeline Lodge Lindbergh.

Credits for the pictures can be found in the back of the book.

Library of Congress Cataloging in Publication Data.

Gill, Brendan, 1914–
    Lindbergh alone.


    1. Lindbergh, Charles Augustus, 1902–1974.
2. Air pilots—United States—Biography. I. Title.
TL540.L5G54      629.13′092′4[B]      76-54288
ISBN 0-15-152401-7

First edition

B  C  D  E

Art Direction: Harris Lewine
Design: Robert Aulicino

A great tradition can be inherited, but
greatness itself must be won
—C.A.L.

The day after which nothing would ever be the same for him was Friday, May 20, 1927. That morning, alone in a little plane powered by a single engine, Charles A. Lindbergh took off from a muddy runway on the outskirts of New York. His destination was Paris. If everything went according to plan—and from earliest childhood he had taken pains to see that everything always went according to plan—he would become the first person in history to fly non-stop from New York to Paris.

For a number of years, Raymond Orteig, a Frenchman who had enjoyed a prosperous career as a hotel proprietor in New York, had been offering a prize of twenty-five thousand dollars to "the first aviator who shall cross the Atlantic in a land or water craft (heavier than air) from Paris or the shores of France to New York, or from New York to Paris or the shores of France, without stop." A few weeks before Lindbergh took off, two celebrated French aviators, Nungesser and Coli, had set out from Paris and had vanished somewhere over the sullen Atlantic. Other aviators, starting from the American side, had suffered one grievous misadventure after another, some of which ended in death.

In 1977, it is all but impossible for us to imagine the heavy weight of unlikelihood borne by Lindbergh's attempt to win the Orteig Prize. The feat of flying non-stop to Paris has long since diminished into so commonplace a passing of a few idle hours aloft that it would never occur to us to mention its being non-stop. Nor would we doubt that, aiming for Paris, we would be sure to reach it. What Lindbergh was the first to do, by an act of superb intelligence and will, millions of us accomplish regularly with the expenditure of no more intelligence and will than is required to purchase a ticket and pack a bag. The once-inimical Atlantic scarcely exists for the contemporary traveler: a glimpse of tame, pewter-colored water at the start or finish of a journey.

In the world's eyes, though not in his own, the odds against Lindbergh in 1927 were prohibitively and perhaps tragically high; from the moment the Spirit of St. Louis started down the runway, lurching under the burden of more gasoline

Roosevelt Field on the morning of the take-off.

than it had ever been called upon to carry, Lindbergh was reckoned to be in desperate danger. Fifty years later, we are statistically no doubt in graver danger driving to Kennedy Airport than we are in flight. In an immense projectile decorated like the lounge of some not very exclusive suburban country club, we are flung through the sky at many hundreds of miles an hour, tens of thousands of feet above the earth. Above the weather as well: somewhere far below us it may be snowing or raining, fierce gales may be lacerating the ocean cauldron, but here we sit eating our pale chicken and waxy chocolate mousse, or watching a movie, or merely dozing over the unread pages of a magazine.

What has this to do with flying as Lindbergh experienced it in his youth and, in after-years, exultantly wrote about it: an encounter on the highest pitch of consciousness between an individual with his assortment of hard-won skills and some impersonal, unknowable God in nature? For as he grew older and thought more deeply about his past, Lindbergh came to believe that the world is riddled with divinity, and to him this divinity manifested itself most openly in the isolation of flight, least openly in the mindless, imposed fraternity of crowds. By an irony that was to be repeated many times throughout his life, the example he set for the rest of us almost always proved to have consequences radically at odds with his intentions—sometimes, indeed, in direct opposition to them. That first New York–to–Paris flight, with its awesome risks coolly faced and outwitted by a single valorous young man, has led to an ever-increasing traffic in the sky above the Atlantic and an ever-decreasing awareness of awe and risk on the part of the army of non-fliers who have followed him. His valor is hard to keep fresh in our minds when the most that we are asked to face and outwit above the Atlantic is boredom.

A fraction of an inch from our eyes as a jet hurtles to or from Paris, on the far side of the thin plastic and metal membrane that encloses us and our scores of fellow-passengers, stretches a heaven of blinding sunlight by day and velvety blue-blackness by night; its temperature is unchangeably ice-cold, its air too thin to breathe. Nearly instant death is out there, but

Lindbergh out over Long Island Sound,
shortly after take-off.

End of the first hour.

our senses reject its presence. We may fear dying in some accident on taking off or landing, but few of us think of dying in the immaculate emptiness of the sky. Our sealed tube is as snug as a night-nursery, and up and down the carpeted aisles proceed in pairs trimly uniformed young women known as flight attendants, offering not only food and drink but, if we wish, a pillow, a blanket, a warm washcloth. There are five different sorts of canned music to choose among and two selections of movies.

This is flying as farce—shrewdly calculated customer relations wearing the conventional thin disguise of solicitude. No wonder that Lindbergh, who spent much of his life helping to develop long-distance commercial flying, found it as a successful operation more and more unsuited to his nature. Aviation had become big business, and as a consultant to Pan American Airways and, later, as a member of its Board of Directors, he was himself a part of big business, and yet he was able to maintain the appearance of being separate from it. The appearance and to some extent the reality: the young loner had learned to work in concert with many types of people, but something in him preserved his solitariness. No matter how big the group or how public its purpose, he remained his own man, invincibly private, making his way along a path of his own devising.

Lindbergh traveled a great deal in the nineteen-fifties and sixties, not as a personage fawned on in the VIP rooms of airports, but as a passenger who seemed at first glance like any other. He traveled first class only when there was no room for him in economy class, and his baggage consisted of as much as he could carry aboard unchecked. Flight for him, as for most of us, had become by then simply a means of saving time; to be trundled in a big jet from continent to continent was scarcely more exhilarating to Lindbergh than to be trundled by bus from New York to Connecticut. Those hours in the air would have been a vexation to him if he had not discovered a way to keep them fruitfully occupied. As soon as he went aboard a plane, he would hunch down in his seat—a white-haired, balding man, no longer recognizable by elderly strangers as the slender "Lindy" of their youth—and give himself up to that labor of writing which had become for him both the best means of shutting a door in the face of the world (few people dare to interrupt a person when he is writing) and the best means of opening a door into himself.

Except for an occasional cat-nap, Lindbergh would rarely lift his eyes from the page as the words flowed on in his strong, legible hand. He was writing at length what he called his "Autobiography of Values." The manuscript amounted to many hundreds of pages, but he was in no hurry to bring it to an end, no hurry to see it in print. If he were to die and the book were to be published posthumously, the title would be sure to make trouble—could there be, after all, such a thing as an autobiography of values? For even if values could be said figuratively to have biographies, could they be said to "write" their own? Wasn't it he who was the writer and not they? Therefore, didn't he mean by his title a meditation on values, told in the form of an autobiography? No matter. In the act of writing, as in the act of making plans for, say, a flight over some vast, as yet unmapped territory, there came a point at which it was necessary to give up weighing one prudent consideration against another. "Autobiography of Values?" The title was crankily, arbitrarily his; it pleased him and it would serve.

Lindbergh and the century were nearly of an age—he was born on February 4, 1902—and each had had much to do with the other. In Frost's phrase, Lindbergh had carried on a lover's quarrel with the world, and he was eager to set down his side of the quarrel. Not in temper but in tranquillity: for a long time, he had been putting in order the matter-of-fact affairs of his outward life and now he was putting in order the affairs of his inward life as well. He wrote in his seventies that old age provided a vantage point from which to look back upon the accumulated values of a lifetime—"with health, one is still close enough to life to feel its surgings and close enough to death to see beyond one's passions." Almost at the moment of writing those words, his health began to fail; he came down with a series of illnesses that seemed at first of little importance but that proved to be the masks of a fatal cancer.

When death neared, in the summer of 1974, Lindbergh was as ready for it as any man could be. He saw it as a test to be taken and passed with honor—the last but not necessarily the hardest of a long lifetime of tests. He bent himself to the ordeal without faltering. He was cheerful and reassuring. He said that he had been close to death many times. He had known what it was to slip back and forth between life and death, and he felt no fear of the moment of passage, or of what might befall thereafter. He would meet death as he had always met life, according to plan.

Of all the ironies that make up Lindbergh's life, none is more startling than the fact that, at the time of his birth, aviation—the means by which he was to become the most famous man of the twentieth century—had yet to exist. He was almost two when the Wright Brothers demonstrated at Kitty Hawk and Kill Devil Hills that powered and directed heavier-than-air flight was possible; he was three in 1905, when the brothers, back home in Dayton, built what history considers to be the first "practical" aircraft. In the early days in Little Falls, Minnesota, Lindbergh never saw a plane; even automobiles were comparative rarities in the small towns of Minnesota in those days, and when a car passed along the winding sandy road beyond the Lindbergh house, everyone rushed to the windows to catch a glimpse of it.

Lindbergh in age was haunted by the number of changes he had experienced at first hand in the comparative brevity of a single lifetime. His paternal grandmother, whom he knew well, vividly recalled to him her terror during the desperate Sioux uprising of 1862, when hundreds of Minnesota settlers were massacred; still further back in time were the stories he heard and cherished about his paternal grandfather, who, before he emigrated to the New World, was an influential member of the Swedish rikstag and a close friend of the King, Charles XV. What a brave man that old August Lindbergh had been! Once, stumbling against the blade of a saw in a mill in Sauk Center he had so mutilated his left arm that it had had to be amputated. The operation had been performed without an anaesthetic, and the family story was that August hadn't uttered so much as a single groan; later, he had rigged up a harness for himself, by means of which he was able to chop wood, cut hay, and carry out other farm tasks as ably as any two-armed man. The life that August Lindbergh led in the fields and pastures of Minnesota was not unlike the life that his ancestors had lived in Sweden for centuries before him—a life close to nature and obedient to its laws. It was a life that young Charles Lindbergh caught the last unself-conscious echoes of when he lived on the farm in Little Falls: a life without electric lights, or telephones, or any sort of mechanical device except a gasoline

pump for drawing water up out of a well. And the man who knew that life knew also, only a few decades later, the life of Cape Canaveral blast-offs and astronauts puttering about in big boots on the gravelly moon.

Lindbergh's childhood on the banks of the Mississippi, roaming the pine and oak woods, swimming and fishing and hunting (he had his own twenty-two-calibre rifle at the age of six and a twelve-gauge shotgun when he was seven), seems to our eyes to be scarcely of the twentieth century at all. In most particulars, it is almost identical to the life that Mark Twain lived some sixty years earlier, in Hannibal, five or six hundred miles downstream from Little Falls. Lindbergh would have been at home in Twain's pre–Civil War environment; certainly he was never altogether at home in ours. With increasing impatience, he tried to escape the tyranny of our incessant technological progress. The future he sought was a kind of past, purged of some of the most terrible of its cruelties. He knew that it was unreasonable to speak of turning back the clock; it was not unreasonable to speak of stopping it and tinkering with it. Failing that, he would do as he had always done; he would move on. The majority of people as they grow older have a tendency to put down roots in some pleasing, familiar place; not Lindbergh. All his life, he had taken care to keep on the move, as if motion were a good in itself. Had he lived into his eighties, he might well have chosen as his last perch a rocky hermitage in a remote mountain fastness in the Philippines or New Guinea, sharing there the life of some pre-literate, stone-age people.

When Lindbergh flew the Atlantic in 1927, he became in our eyes the avatar of a new breed of American—one who seemed cheerfully at ease, as most of the rest of us were not, with the intricate technical wonders pouring daily from our laboratories and factories. He stood for the promises of applied science as a young poet might stand for the promises of the word. He had a thrilling gospel to preach and he preached it in good faith, to millions of people throughout the world, both by uttering it in brief speeches and by the example of his little plane in flight. Aviation was an intrinsic good, which would prove a valuable servant to mankind. Even as it was increasing

Evangeline Lindbergh and Charles.

Grandfather Land gave Charles a .22 rifle when he was six and rigged up a target-practice area for him behind the Land house.

Charles and his hound-dog Spot on the west bank of the Mississippi just below the Lindbergh house.

a nation's commercial prosperity, it would draw hostile strangers into brotherhood.

In the twenties, it was still possible to believe many of
these things. The universal good that aviation seemed capable
of bestowing on mankind had received only one substantial
challenge: its use in the First World War. Planes had rained
bombs indiscriminately upon the earth, not only over battle-
fields but over cities as well. They had proved admirably adroit
extensions of artillery, and designers and technicians would no
doubt quickly overcome the drawback of their being unable to
carry heavy loads over long distances; then what an addition to
the art of war they would make! Meanwhile, the newspapers
and magazines were full of accounts of the exploits of the
aces—those gallant young fliers whose aerial combats put
everyone in mind of the joustings and tournaments of the far-
off Middle Ages. Few people could find it in their hearts to object to personal combat in the sky. True, men died in these
spectacular, caracoling gun-fights, but their deaths were a con-
sequence of a defeat suffered in what amounted to a fair contest—they had had their chance and they had lost, precisely as
they would have expected to do in any sporting event on the
ground. As soon as the war was over, the surviving aces on
both sides would get together and shake hands and reminisce;
they were all gentlemanly heroes together.

Lindbergh as a teen-aged boy in Little Falls daydreamed
of being among the aces. As soon as he was eighteen, he
would sign up with the U.S. Flying Service and become a
scout; soon he would be a Rickenbacker, a Richthofen. In fact,
the First World War ended too soon for Lindbergh to take part
in it; his daydream had to wait until the Second World War to
be fulfilled. In 1944, as a civilian "observer" and therefore fla-
grantly against all the rules, Lindbergh flew no fewer than fifty
combat missions, dropping bombs on gun emplacements
and, on one occasion, engaging a Japanese pilot, whom he
shot down somewhere over South Borneo. He would have
been bitterly disappointed not to have had these tastes of combat; he rejoiced to pit his flying skills against other people's,
and no wonder—by common consent he was the greatest flier

that ever lived.

If it is ironic for a man to be older than his métier, it is still more ironic for him to live long enough to wish that the métier had never come into existence. For years, Lindbergh served as a consultant to the Secretary of the Air Force, and in the course of his duties he helped to reorganize the Strategic Air Command.

> Although I could find no wise alternative [he wrote in his "Autobiography of Values"], each year that I worked on weapons development left me more concerned about our future. It appeared to me that our civilization involved a negative evolution for life, and that the security we were building for today and tomorrow led toward eventual catastrophe....I came to accept that even a catastrophic war was probably not the greatest danger confronting modern man. Civil technology vied with military technology in breaking down human heredity and the natural environment. Every day, increasing numbers of bulldozers and trucks tore into mountains, slashed through forests, leaving far greater scars on the earth's surface than those created by bombs. Gases from civil vehicles polluted our atmosphere. Wastes from civil factories poisoned our rivers, lakes, and seas. Civil aircraft laid every spot on earth open to the ravages of commerce.... What was the prospect for mankind?

Plainly, for Lindbergh the prospect seemed dark indeed, but he had learned something as a young aviator that caused him to square his shoulders and face the darkness instead of retreating from it. Barnstorming throughout the West and, later, flying the mail from St. Louis to Chicago, he had reached the conclusion that the best way to cope with danger was to keep in continuous, intimate contact with it. Now, feeling that civilization as he had known it was in grave danger, he plunged with his usual energy and high spirits into the task of rescuing it. He mastered the history of the great, fallen civilizations of the past; he traveled around the globe to measure with his own eyes the size of the threatened disaster. Always he was taking notes; Los Angeles, when he had first visited it as a boy of fourteen, had been a lovely city, basking in clear air and sunlight, surrounded by orchards and little farms, framed by the ocean and a distant semicircle of mountains. "When I flew over it in a

Pan American jet-transport fifty years later," he wrote, "the orchards and farms had vanished. The city itself had expanded to the distant mountains and spilled over them into the valleys beyond. Smoky haze screened off the sunlight that once bathed farms, yards, and streets."

Hong Kong, Rio de Janeiro, Tokyo, Rome: the story was everywhere the same. The slender young man who had urged more air routes, more airports, more international trade was now the aging man who urged us to be content with less of everything—fewer babies, fewer cars, fewer weapons, fewer luxuries. It was remarkable, he said, what you could learn to live without. He himself enjoyed traveling for weeks on end with, for luggage, a couple of drip-dry shirts, a couple of pairs of drip-dry socks, a necktie that, being worn every day in a different city, wouldn't be noticed to be always the same tie. He became an ardent champion of the Agta shelter, used by the Agta people on the northeastern coast of Luzon. The shelter consists of a flat framework of poles, onto which big leaves are laced. The shelter is slightly higher and slightly wider than the height of a tall man. Braced up at an angle by a single pole butted into the sand, it protects its occupants—often an entire family—against wind, rain, and sun. In one of his notes, he wrote, "I wish I could always leave my civilization behind at night, to sleep under an Agta shelter on a Luzon beach." He was carefree at that moment, happy in spirit, but the darkness of the prospect was real and so was the danger. Valiantly he embraced them. In 1974, a few weeks before his death, he wrote in the solemn cadences of a last testament: "I do not want to be a member of the generation that through blindness and indifference destroys the quality of life on our planet."

Where had he sprung from, this extraordinary man? It was a question being asked all over the world on the morning of May 22, 1927, while Lindbergh lay sleeping in the United States Embassy building in Paris, and it was still being asked in August, 1974, while he lay dying at his island home in Hawaii. After almost fifty years of intense public scrutiny, Lindbergh remained a figure baffling at close range even to his admirers, who did what they could to conceal their disappointment.

Because they believed Lindbergh to be a great man, their bafflement could be said at the very least to serve as a sort of affidavit to his greatness. For it is a paradox characteristic of great men that the nearer we come to them the more mysterious they may seem to be. The mystery is rarely of their making; it is not that they withhold the truth about themselves but that they are unable to grant us access to it. What Lindbergh's admirers feared wasn't that, seen more clearly, he would appear less great to them; what they feared was that on the far side of their bafflement waited something unknown and of high value, which they might never come into possession of.

Nobody ever vaulted to fame more quickly than Lindbergh, or kept his fame more securely as the first occasion for it grew dim. There were young people in the nineteen-fifties and sixties who had never heard of his New York–to–Paris flight; to them, he was celebrated as a conservationist (the man who helped to prevent the extinction of the monkey-eating eagle: that much they knew), as perhaps to their parents he was celebrated as the military expert who had confidently predicted the defeat of England in the Second World War and had been branded a near-traitor by President Roosevelt. Whatever the means, whether favorable or unfavorable, by which his fame was preserved over the years, there he stood, the most conspicuous and elusive and forthright and secretive of Americans.

An enigma to us and almost certainly an enigma to himself—in the long manuscript of his "Autobiography of Values," it is his own nature that he marches round and seeks to come to grips with, often in vain. Out of a prodigious memory for physical details, he can summon up the facts of his life on what amounts to a daily and even an hourly basis, but when it comes to the Proustian heartland of feelings and motives, recollection tends to grow thin. As a man of science, he was irresistibly drawn to examining the exterior world and the means by which it works, but he wrote little about the mind and the means by which it works, and the little that he wrote is gingerly. His body in all its particulars was a private matter; he was fascinated by the way it responded to physical stimuli—heat, cold, fatigue, and the like—but when it came to the emotions his explorations, even in his private journals, were tentative. There was a tradition among the Lindberghs of making no outward show of emotion, whether of joy or grief, and an inward show appears to have been equally difficult for them.

No American has ever professed a greater desire for privacy than Lindbergh did, and few Americans have lived a life more persistently public. When he met and fell in love with and married Anne Spencer Morrow—their wedding day was May 27, 1929—it was obvious that she was every bit as shy as he and every bit as determined to maintain her privacy, and yet a curious thing: between them over the years they produced something like twelve or fourteen books, all of them highly autobiographical. Shyness and privacy are shields, but they are also weapons, as readily capable of imposing themselves on the world as the most arrant acts of exhibitionism. Despite their instinctive aversion to publicity, the Lindberghs would do whatever they could to keep their lives from being swallowed up in vulgar journalistic fabrications. They were circumspect Boswells, with no scandals and little gossip to relate in their voluminous diaries, letters, and narratives; their intention was to let history see them as they really were, through their own eyes, rather than through the eyes of the shoddy, inaccurate press. It was an intention innocent and admirable and doomed to fail, but the writing went on.

The question of where Lindbergh had sprung from began to be answered with increasing irresponsibility the day the newly finished Spirit of St. Louis took off from San Diego. The

In flying togs.

plane had been designed by Donald A. Hall, the chief engineer of Ryan Airlines, Inc., according to specifications drawn up by Lindbergh; Hall and Lindbergh had personally overseen its construction, which was completed in the exceptionally short period of eight weeks. The men in the Ryan factory worked on the plane night and day, seven days a week, some of them going as long as twenty-four hours without rest. No plane like it existed anywhere in the world; it was a beautiful, silvery toy, just under twenty-eight feet long and with a wing-span of forty-six feet. It was built of steel tubing and spruce wood and piano wire and cotton fabric, tautened and made air- and watertight with dope, and it had a nine-cylinder Wright Whirlwind engine, estimated to be able to run for nine thousand hours without a breakdown. (Lindbergh was figuring that he might need as much as forty hours to cover the thirty-six hundred miles between New York and Paris; as far as the engine was concerned, the margin of safety seemed ample.) The plane had three gasoline tanks, with a total capacity of four hundred and fifty gallons. Empty, it weighed twenty-one hundred and fifty pounds; loaded, it weighed fifty-one hundred and thirty-five pounds. Most of this weight was gasoline; of the rest, Lindbergh himself, fully clothed, weighed a hundred and seventy pounds, and there were forty pounds of indispensable, miscellaneous gear. On paper, the little plane promised to fly just over four thousand miles non-stop, at an average speed of something around a hundred miles an hour; the margin of safety, this time for unfavorable weather and errors in navigation, again seemed ample. The plane had cost Lindbergh and his nine St. Louis backers less than fourteen thousand dollars.

Lindbergh made a record-breaking, non-stop flight east from San Diego to St. Louis and, the very next day, a second record-breaking flight, from St. Louis to New York. Until then, he had been merely a name, often misspelled (Lindberg, Lineburg, Lundbergh), in news items about Byrd, Chamberlin, and the other well-known fliers competing for the Orteig Prize. When he touched down at Curtiss Field, on Long Island, the news of the sensationally speedy little plane and its blue-eyed, tousle-haired young pilot had already caught the imagination of the public. As Lindbergh was later to write, recollecting after many years the astonishment and dismay he felt during his first overwhelming encounter with the public and the press, "The moment I step outside the hangar I'm surrounded by people and protected by police. Somebody shouts my name, and immediately I'm surrounded by a crowd. Even at the hotel, newspapermen fill the lobby and watch the entrance so carefully that I can't walk around the block without being followed. There's never a free moment except when I'm in my room."

Soon it turned out that Lindbergh was no safer from interruption in the hotel room than he was on the street. One evening, waiting impatiently for word that the weather over the Atlantic had begun to clear, he and some friends were going over details of the flight when the door to his room burst open and two men strode into the room carrying press cameras. When his friends asked the men what they wanted, they replied that they had been ordered to get pictures of "Lucky Lindy" shaving and sitting on his bed in his pajamas. Lindbergh and his friends thrust the men bodily out of the room and locked the door. Lindbergh was trembling with indignation. How dared they behave in that fashion, he wondered. How <u>dared</u> they? As for "Lucky Lindy," how he hated to be called that! Never in his life had he depended upon luck for anything; for that matter, never in his life had he been called "Lindy." It was a nickname based on the need in newspaper headlines for a catchy brevity. The papers might have fallen back upon his initials, reducing him for their purposes to the briefest possible C.A.L., but those were letters reserved for the President of the United States, Calvin Coolidge. Mocking Coolidge's habitual bleak stiffness of demeanor, the tabloids always referred to him jauntily as CAL. No, "Lindy" it would have to be, and when space permitted the fatuous "Lucky" would be added to provide alliteration. For variety, from time to time he would also be called "The Kid Flyer" and "The Flyin' Fool."

For the first time, Lindbergh was experiencing that dehumanization of people which is the special skill of popular

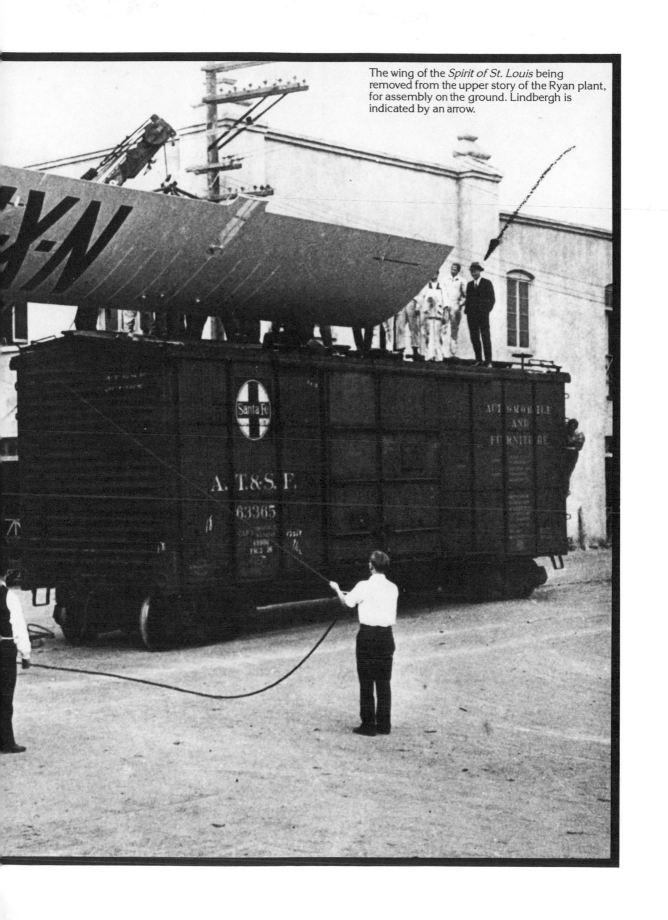

The wing of the *Spirit of St. Louis* being removed from the upper story of the Ryan plant, for assembly on the ground. Lindbergh is indicated by an arrow.

journalism. The press had little interest in who he was and still less interest in what the flight meant to him and might mean to the country and the world. Day after day, with a hit-or-miss recklessness that nobody would ever take the trouble to examine (who cared whether yesterday's inside stories were true or false?), reporters fumbled their way toward a Lindbergh whom the public would be eager to read about—a Lindbergh who would sell papers. Their task was made easier for them because they had so little to go on. Unlike the over-publicized Commander Byrd, whose big three-motored Fokker had been expected for months to be the first plane across the Atlantic, Lindbergh was a new figure in New York; the press could do whatever it wished with him, or so it thought.

If the press had little to go on, that little was choice: Lindbergh was tall and slender, with a pleasing seriousness of manner, which could be instantly transformed into playfulness by a radiant smile. Although he was twenty-five and on several occasions had faced death both on the ground and in the air, he struck almost everyone who met him as an unmarked boy. The boylike quality was something deeper than mere boyishness; it sprang in large part from the indubitable purity of his character. He neither smoked nor drank, and it was impossible to imagine him as a womanizer. On the contrary, he was manly and virginal, as a boy can be manly and virginal, and reporters—most of them chain-smokers, hard drinkers, and casual in their sexual relations—were genuinely drawn to him by their unlikeness to him. Looking up into those clear eyes, listening to that eager voice, one felt sure that here was someone who would never cheat, or lie, or take unfair advantage. He was assuredly the All-American Boy, and then something more. It was the something more—the proud and passionate inner man, bent on self-fulfillment at whatever cost—that the press got wrong and continued to get wrong throughout his life.

Lindbergh himself thought that he knew what the reporters were after in those long, watchful May days of 1927, and he marveled at their professional slovenliness: when facts were so abundant, why did they not make some slight effort to ascer-

Lindbergh and his mother a few days before the flight.

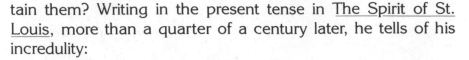 

tain them? Writing in the present tense in The Spirit of St. Louis, more than a quarter of a century later, he tells of his incredulity:

> Depending on which paper I pick up, I find that I was born in Minnesota, that I was born in Michigan, that I was born in Nebraska; that I learned to fly at Omaha, that I learned to fly at Lincoln, that I learned to fly at San Antonio. . . The Spirit of St. Louis is ready to take off, but my route to Paris is still covered with fog and storm. These have been the most extraordinary days I have ever spent; and I can't call them very pleasant. Life has become too strange and hectic. The attention of the entire country is centered on the flight to Paris, and most of all on me—because I'm going alone, because I'm young, because I'm a "dark horse." Papers in every city and village are headlining my name and writing articles about me. Newspaper, radio, and motion-picture publicity has brought people crowding out to Curtiss and Roosevelt Fields until the Nassau County police are faced with a major traffic problem. Seventy-five hundred came last Saturday, the New York Times said. On Sunday there were thirty thousand. . . .

In the following paragraph, one sees how careful Lindbergh was to distinguish between "our" and "my." The flight as a project he shared equally with his St. Louis backers, but his dreams and his reputation as a pilot belonged to him alone:

> Up to date, our project has been successful beyond my wildest dreams. We've brought the attention to St. Louis that we planned. We've helped focus everybody's eyes on aviation and its future. We've shown what kind of flights a modern plane can make; and my reputation as a pilot has been established. The New York Times is going to buy the story of my flight and syndicate it throughout the country. All this is very satisfactory. But there are disturbing elements too. The way the tabloid people acted when my mother came left me with no respect for them. They didn't care how much they hurt her feelings or frightened her about my flight, as long as they got their pictures and their stories. Did she know what a dangerous trip I was undertaking? they asked. Did she realize how many older and more experienced aviators had been killed in its attempt? They wanted her to describe her sensations for their readers. They demanded that we embrace for their cameras and say goodbye. When we refused, one paper had two other people go through the mo-

Just before the flight.

tions, and substituted photographs of our heads for theirs—composite pictures, they call them.

It was thanks to the press that the project—with the flight itself not yet undertaken!—had proved successful "beyond my wildest dreams." Lindbergh saw clearly that he was using reporters to gain his ends and he saw with equal clarity that they were using him to gain theirs, but the bargain became every day a harder one for him to live up to.

After the flight, a mythology would be erected upon the premise that young Lindbergh had passed in those first summer days of 1927 from a naïve readiness to make friends with reporters to a grim, lifelong antagonism to them. Nothing of the kind: he was far from ignorant of the nature of the press at the beginning of his fame, and in middle age and old age, although opposed to personal publicity of any kind, he welcomed publicity for the causes he championed—how were such causes to be championed in our society, except through publicity? It may have been true that he went to Maui to die partly in order not to die in big headlines in New York, but a short while earlier he had encouraged headlines for a threatened species of whale, a threatened tribe of primitive people.

At the start of his flying career, as a college dropout barnstorming through the West and South, Lindbergh had much to gain from free publicity; when he and his buddies turned up in a town to offer plane rides ("a good ride for five dollars"), or put on exhibitions of parachute-jumping, wing-walking, and other stunts, a few lines in the local paper would help to bring out the crowds. Even then, of course, and especially when things went wrong, reporters would twist the facts askew in order to heighten the supposed danger of flying and make daredevil Lindbergh and his colleagues appear much more heroic than they believed themselves to be. One day in 1923, Lindbergh was flying to Shakopee, Minnesota, to meet his father. Charles A. Lindbergh, Sr., was seeking—in vain, as it turned out—to run for United States Senator on the Farmer-Labor ticket, in a special election necessitated by the death of the incumbent, Knute Nelson. Charles's intention was to fly his father around the state from rally to rally, in a then novel demonstration of the efficiency of aircraft in political campaigns.

Lindbergh was flying a Curtiss Jenny—a little trainer plane left over from the First World War, which, equipped with a new engine, Lindbergh had recently purchased for five hundred dollars at an Army depot in Georgia. On his way to Shakopee, he ran into continuous thunderstorms; he tells the story of his subsequent misadventure in We, his first essay into autobiography, which he wrote in great haste in July, 1927, shortly

A typical broadside of the old barnstorming days.

SOUTHERN ILLINOIS HARD ROAD BASEBALL
ASSOCIATION CARTERVILLE TEAM PRESENTS

Vera May Dunlap's

# Flying Circus

In conjunction with their opening game

## Sat. & Sun., May 9 & 10

At Carterville Base Ball and Aviation Field

1 MILE SO. OF CARTERVILLE AT CROSS ROADS

### Carries Mills vs. Carterville

By special arrangements Vera May Dunlap will appear
IN PERSON and will positively stand erect on top of the
upper wing of the airplane without any visible means of
support whatsoever while her pilot loops the loop, defying
all laws of gravitation. Miss Dunlap carries with her a
fleet of airplanes under the personal direction of Capt.
Frank T. Dunn, the Canadian Ace. The only flier who
has successfully looped the bridge on a navigable stream.
Also Herbert Budd in the swing of death. T. Gurney the
fastest wing walker and aerial performer in the world.
Enslow, Hissel, Mann, Armstrong and Brown, pilots. Last
but not least is Lt. Chas. A. Lindberg who saved his life by
jumping from an aerial collision on March 6, 1925 in Kelly
Field, Texas. He is now in the U. S. Air Service and will
positively be in Carterville May 9-10. Herbert Budd will
change from the top of one plane to another without any
rope ladder. Admission to the ball game, including the
airplane circus will be

## 50 cents

The gates will be open at 10:00 A. M. Parking space for
cars free. Miss Dunlap also has three passenger carrying
planes with licensed pilots for those wishing to ride. Price
to ride $3.00. Look for airplane distributing programs as
some will contain free riding and admission tickets.

Carterville Herald Print.

Lindbergh's first plane was a Jenny, left over from the World War. Here he has just made a forced landing near Savage, Minnesota.

after his triumphal return to the States:

I found Shakopee covered by a cloudburst and in flying around waiting for the storm to pass so that I could land I got into a heavy shower near Savage. One of the cylinders cut out, and I was circling preparatory to landing in a clover field when two more stopped firing. I was flying at less than a two hundred foot altitude and losing that rapidly. It was necessary to land immediately but the only choice of landing places lay between a swamp and high trees. I took the swamp and cut the throttle. When the wheels touched earth they rolled about twenty feet, sank in to the spreader bar, and we nosed over.

The rudder did not quite touch the swamp grass and the plane stopped after passing through three-quarters of a circle, with the radiator cap and top wing resting on the ground. I was hanging on the safety belt but when I tried to open the clasp with one hand, holding on with the other to keep from falling out on my head, I found it to be jammed. After several futile attempts to open it I reverted to the two strap buckles at the end of the belt to release myself from the cockpit.

All this required not more than two or three minutes.

After getting out of the cockpit I inspected the plane carefully. Again there was little actual damage. The propeller was badly cracked and would have to be replaced; there was a crack in the spreader bar which required winding with strong cord. Otherwise the plane was in perfect condition, although splashed with mud.

For once there was no one in sight and I made my way through the swamp to the nearest farmhouse. On the way I found that there was solid ground along the edge of the swamp less than one hundred yards from the plane from which I could take off.

The farmer had seen the plane pass over in the rain and was on his way down towards the swamp when I met him. He informed me that it was not possible to get horses through the mire out to the ship and that he had no idea of how I was to get it back to hard sod again.

I borrowed a rope from him to use in pulling the tail back to a normal position and we started back to the swamp.

Meanwhile it seems that two boys had seen me land, and when I did not emerge from the cockpit immediately, had run to Savage with the news that "an aviator had landed upside down in the swamp" and that they had "gone up and felt of his neck and that it was stiff and he was stone dead."

I had flown over the town in the rain only a few minutes before, and as in those days it was not difficult for anyone to believe anything about an airplaine, the town promptly locked its doors and came crawling and wading through the swamp. The older inhabitants followed the railroad track around its edge and by the time I returned with the farmer and a rope there were enough townspeople to solve my problem by carrying the ship back onto solid ground.

They were undoubtedly much disappointed at having come so far on a false alarm but turned willingly to help me get the ship out of the swamp.

The next edition of one of the Minneapolis papers carried the following item, which typically exemplifies what has been the average man's knowledge of aeronautics:

### AIRPLANE CRASHES NEAR SAVAGE

Charles A. Lindbergh, son of ex-Congressman Lindbergh, crashed near Savage, Minnesota, this morning. He was flying in his plane three hundred feet above the ground when it suddenly went into a nose dive and landed on its propeller in a swamp. Lindbergh says he will be flying again in three days.

Now, to the general public the newspaper account would seem a harmless exaggeration of the facts. Lindbergh hadn't been flying at three hundred feet and the plane hadn't "suddenly" gone into a nose dive, or indeed into any kind of dive; it hadn't, in Lindbergh's view, crashed—it had simply made a forced landing at no great risk to him or to the plane. Non-fliers in those days regarded flying as a highly perilous and therefore terrifying activity; Lindbergh wished it to be seen to be no more dangerous than riding a motorcycle. If one took precautions, if one anticipated trouble...but then newspaper reporters and newspaper readers had no interest in precautions. They wanted excitement. They wanted heroes, especially heroes facing almost certain death.

In the years that followed, Lindbergh was often to be confronted by the press, for despite his youth and modesty he had a penchant for doing things that called attention to himself. As a barnstormer, he was exceptionally bold; as an aviator, he was exceptionally skillful; and as a person he had exceptional good

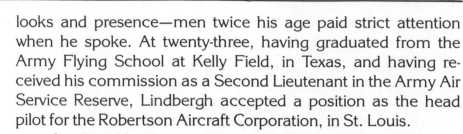 

looks and presence—men twice his age paid strict attention when he spoke. At twenty-three, having graduated from the Army Flying School at Kelly Field, in Texas, and having received his commission as a Second Lieutenant in the Army Air Service Reserve, Lindbergh accepted a position as the head pilot for the Robertson Aircraft Corporation, in St. Louis.

Lindbergh's title and the name of the company sounded grander than they were. There were only two other pilots employed by Robertson—Army buddies of Lindbergh's named Love and Allen, whom Lindbergh had recruited—and the company itself was of little commercial importance; it had been formed by two brothers, both fliers in the First World War, and they had hired their three young pilots subject to the company's winning a United States Post Office contract to fly mail between St. Louis and Chicago. The government, which had introduced a sketchy air-mail service in 1918 and had extended it from coast to coast in 1920, had decided by 1925 to add a number of feeder-lines along the way; of these, one of the most important would be the line linking St. Louis and Chicago.

The Robertsons won the contract and asked Lindbergh to lay out the route between the two cities. In April, 1926, Lindbergh flew the first sacks of mail from St. Louis to Chicago. It was a big aviation story for that day, and the result was that Lindbergh had to face a good deal of interrogation by the press. The reporters were tiresome enough, but they were nothing like as big a nuisance as the photographers, some of whom worked for newspapers and magazines and others of whom worked for the then popular movie-newsreel companies. Reporters took notes and rushed off to write their stories, whether accurately or inaccurately; photographers hung around waiting for something to happen, and no matter how patiently one accommodated oneself to their needs, they remained unsatisfied.

Lindbergh wrote a long letter to his mother describing the day the air-mail flights began and expressing his irritation with the "darned" photographers. (The "darned" is characteristic, not alone in letters to his mother and not alone in his youth. Lindbergh was never one to employ strong language. Among

Second Lieutenant Charles A. Lindbergh, March, 1925.

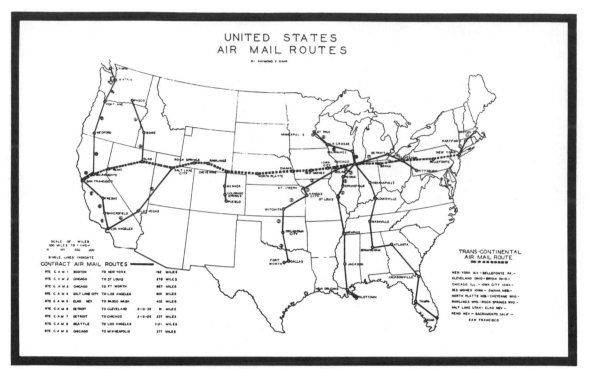

### UNITED STATES AIR MAIL ROUTES

BY RAYMOND V BAHR

The air-mail routes that were being flown in 1926. Lindbergh laid out the route between St. Louis and Chicago.

In 1926 Lindbergh inaugurated the air-mail route between St. Louis and Chicago. Here the first sacks are being stowed in the plane, a refurbished De Havilland.

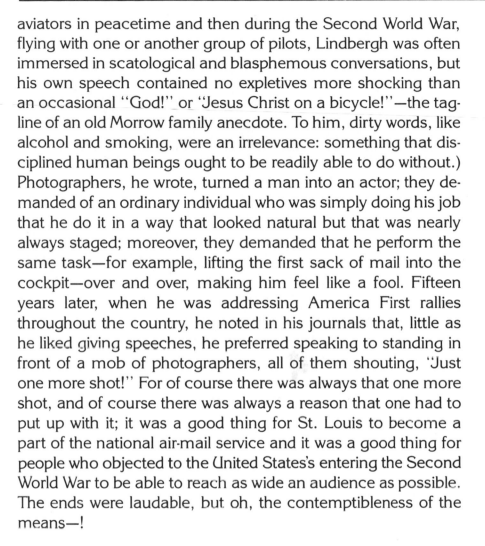

aviators in peacetime and then during the Second World War, flying with one or another group of pilots, Lindbergh was often immersed in scatological and blasphemous conversations, but his own speech contained no expletives more shocking than an occasional "God!" or "Jesus Christ on a bicycle!"—the tagline of an old Morrow family anecdote. To him, dirty words, like alcohol and smoking, were an irrelevance: something that disciplined human beings ought to be readily able to do without.) Photographers, he wrote, turned a man into an actor; they demanded of an ordinary individual who was simply doing his job that he do it in a way that looked natural but that was nearly always staged; moreover, they demanded that he perform the same task—for example, lifting the first sack of mail into the cockpit—over and over, making him feel like a fool. Fifteen years later, when he was addressing America First rallies throughout the country, he noted in his journals that, little as he liked giving speeches, he preferred speaking to standing in front of a mob of photographers, all of them shouting, "Just one more shot!" For of course there was always that one more shot, and of course there was always a reason that one had to put up with it; it was a good thing for St. Louis to become a part of the national air-mail service and it was a good thing for people who objected to the United States's entering the Second World War to be able to reach as wide an audience as possible. The ends were laudable, but oh, the contemptibleness of the means—!

At Curtiss Field, a few days before he took off for Paris, Lindbergh made a couple of test flights, on the last of which the tail skid of the <u>Spirit of St. Louis</u> was broken. The accident happened because a number of photographers ran out onto the field and got in Lindbergh's way. "The most annoying thing," he wrote, "was that, instead of having a penalty to pay for violating the field regulations, the cameramen got a more valuable picture—and the reporters had 'a better story.' That seemed to be all they cared about. As far as I could tell, the fact that I damaged my plane to keep from hitting somebody didn't bother them a bit. Most reporters omitted that from their accounts. 'So terrific was his speed in landing that he slightly damaged the machine's tail skid. Undismayed by the accident, which he considered trivial, Lindbergh hopped out wearing a broad smile: "Boys, she's ready and rarin' to go!" he said.' That's how one of the next day's articles went. These fellows must think I'm a cowpuncher, just transferred to aviation."

Not only would reporters favor a good story over an accurate one—their idea of a good story often prompted them to invent a new Lindbergh, different from one day to the next from the actual man they spoke to and watched moving quietly about the hangar and field. Before the flight, they portrayed him as a lanky bumpkin out of the West; after the flight, they portrayed him as a Viking god, with "the look of eagles in his eyes." He was somebody far more interesting than either of those glib caricatures. Moreover, he was aware of his own interestingness. He did not undervalue himself. He came from a long line of unusually gifted and intelligent forebears and he perceived without vanity that he would prove worthy of them. "A great tradition," he wrote, in his <u>Wartime Journals</u>, "can be inherited, but greatness itself must be won." Almost from infancy, he had set himself the task of winning that greatness.

Lindbergh took seriously the Platonic dictum that the unexamined life is not worth living; still, there were times when he found the principle easier to respect than to follow. What was surely the single most important event in the forming of his character—the early breakup of his parents' marriage—he glanced at again and again throughout his life, always to turn away from it in filial distress. Though he would go so far as to speak of the failed marriage as a tragic event, he was reluctant to speculate on the causes of the tragedy. Perhaps he was too much the child of each parent to pass judgment on them, in part because passing judgment would amount to a form of taking sides; or perhaps he did indeed pass judgment and was then unable to pronounce sentence. The posthumous punishment of parents is a task that sons and daughters find it irresistible to contemplate but hard to carry out; some primordial superstition nearly always stays our hand.

The fact is that the death of parents, especially if they have succeeded in reaching middle age, is far from being an altogether sad event. It releases us from a bondage of piety that has many drawbacks as well as many rewards; behind the authentic anguish of loss, we feel an increment of strength that, under other circumstances, we might be inclined to describe as joy. We are invested with an energy different from any we have known before, and some of that energy goes at once into the finally permissible family daydream, whose subject is: what were they like, those two? What were they <u>really</u> like, together? It is a daydream that for most of us can last a lifetime; we carry it to our graves, ruefully aware that for our children the latest cycle in the long daydream is just coming to birth.

Lindbergh survived his mother by twenty years and his father by almost forty, but in all that time he had little to reveal about their relationship. Well into old age, he cherished a pious hope that somehow or other, in spite of everything, they had gone on caring for each other. He said he believed this to be the case; but then even in age we go on believing what it is useful for us to believe, or, rather, what it is intolerable for us not to believe. Lindbergh had performed an astonishing feat: as the

(Top, left) Lindbergh's grandfather, August Lindbergh.

(Top, right) Lindbergh's mother, Evangeline Land, as a schoolgirl in Detroit.

(Bottom, left) Charles A. Lindbergh, Sr. in 1901, the year of his marriage to Evangeline Land.

(Above) Evangeline seated in an oak tree in Edgewater Park, Chicago in 1898.

Charles and C.A.

only child of alienated parents, he had managed to bestow a similar trust and affection upon both. He saw clearly that he was the single superb achievement of their briefly mingled lives and for his own sake as well as theirs he wanted the gift of himself to have been worth the making.

Charles A. Lindbergh, Sr., was almost as remarkable a man as Charles, Jr.—save in the degree of his fame, perhaps equally remarkable. Like most self-made men, he did everything in his power to create a son in his own image and, unlike most self-made men, he succeeded. If a success of this kind is always rare, what is rarer still is for the success to repeat itself in one family for several generations. C.A., as the senior Lindbergh was always called, was himself the scion of a formidably ambitious father, who treated his son Charles as that son was to treat his sons...the span is a long one, embracing well over a hundred and fifty years, and the tradition is by no means in disrepute among the present generation.

August Lindbergh, born in Sweden in 1808, had risen by his own efforts from the peasantry into the land-owning middle class. At thirty-nine, he was elected to Parliament and for a time served as secretary to the Crown Prince, Charles Augustus. In Parliament, he was considered a high-principled reformer by his admirers and a dangerous radical by his adversaries; it was the latter who eventually arranged (according to a family story) to implicate him in a trumped-up financial scandal. In part because of the scandal and in part because, his first wife having died, August had recently taken a bride, he decided to retire from Parliament and begin a new life in the wilderness of Minnesota. His colleagues in Parliament presented him with a gold medal as a token of their esteem, and off he went—a fifty-two-year-old man with a twenty-year-old wife and a one-year-old son, whom he had named Charles Augustus after his good friend the newly crowned Charles XV.

When August started homesteading near Melrose, Minnesota, not far from Sauk Center, one of the first things he did was to trade his gold medal for a plow. So goes another family story, but how unreliable these stories are, even among such stern truth-tellers as the Lindberghs! August was a hard-headed man, and nobody could have persuaded him to exchange a valuable piece of gold for a plow, worth in those days a few dollars at most. Is it possible that the medal wasn't of gold? Or is it possible that there wasn't, in fact, any medal? A third family story about August, also implausible: on coming to America, he had changed his name from Ola Mansson to August Lindbergh and long afterwards he gave as his reason for doing so the fact that there were already so many Manssons in his part of Sweden. But if that were the reason, why had he not changed his name years earlier? Moreover, since he was to be henceforth in America, what difference did it make how many Manssons there might be in Sweden? Maybe August changed his name because of the scandal, or maybe he changed it because his new wife wanted to be the first Mrs. Lindbergh instead of the second Mrs. Mansson. It was a trifling matter—fixed patronymics were a comparative novelty in the Sweden of those days and one was free to adopt or discard names at will.

August and his wife had many children, with the result that their first-born was early on his own. Like his son after him, C.A. at six was already in possession of a gun, and it was his appointed task to keep the family table supplied with game—deer, partridge, duck, wild turkey, and the like. He grew up to be an unusually handsome, unusually self-reliant young man, who loved swimming and hunting and solitude and who strongly disliked school. In words that Charles might have echoed, C.A. once wrote, "When it comes time for the boy to go to school he does not take his mind there with him. He is ordered to go and he goes, but his mind goes back to where his sports have been. If one can't take his mind to school with him, school is a decidedly uninteresting place." At twenty, he began belatedly to apply himself to his studies. After a year in a local academy, he entered the University of Michigan Law School and in two years received his degree, in the class of 1884. Having read law for a year with a judge in St. Cloud, he opened an office in the prosperous lumbering town of Little Falls, on the banks of the Mississippi some hundred miles north of

Minneapolis.

C.A. was as fiercely high-principled as his father and would never agree to defend a person whom he believed to be in the wrong. Like his father, by merit he made his way up from extreme poverty into the land-owning middle class. He built and sold a number of houses in Little Falls, purchased and sold nearby farmlands, and served on the boards of directors of a couple of local banks, where he championed the unpopular cause of granting farmers mortgages at reasonable rates. He studied economics and became, like August, increasingly radical in his politics as he grew older. At the same time, he cherished the privileges of the bourgeoisie. He met and married a leading belle in Little Falls and had three daughters by her; one of the daughters died and then his wife suddenly died, at thirty-one, of an inoperable cancer. The year was 1895. Overnight, C.A. had been transformed into that classic figure of the popular novels of the late nineteenth century—a good-looking, wealthy, honorable, and grieving widower in his middle thirties, with two motherless children to raise.

In the slang phrase of the day, C.A. was a catch, but his grief was genuine and it was some years before he consented to be caught. And then it happened, again as in a novel, that the girl who caught him was herself a catch—a welcome stranger in every way to the stolid Swedish conventionalities of Little Falls. She had a degree as a Bachelor of Science from the University of Michigan, class of 1898, and at twenty-four she had come to Little Falls to teach chemistry in the local high school under the romantic misapprehension—she was singularly young for her age—that she would be living the life of a pioneer, in a mining village surrounded by painted Indians and wild beasts of the forest. She was said to have been the prettiest girl of her time at the University of Michigan and she was very spirited—she had had an Irish grandmother and she liked to detect in herself (and afterwards in her son) evidences of an Irish deviltry. Her name was Evangeline Lodge Land, and her ancestry was even more distinguished than that of C.A. Her father, Dr. Charles H. Land, was a celebrated dentist and inventor in Detroit, of an old family that had helped to settle Ontario; her mother, after whom she was named, was the daughter of a prominent Detroit physician and pharmacist. Two of her mother's brothers were also physicians and a third brother eventually became Mayor of Detroit. The Lands and the Lodges were a lively, bantering family group and they were very proud of young "Eva," with her university degree and her adventurous nature.

Evangeline and C.A. were both boarding at the same hotel in Little Falls and soon they struck up an acquaintance. Evangeline was an ardent writer of letters, and her mother, with whom she was always on terms of eager affection, was kept fully informed of her interest in the "older" man—C.A. was seventeen years older than Evangeline. In September, 1900, she wrote to Mrs. Land:

> The widower walked home from church this morning with me and another girl named Miss Cooper. Hem! I don't want him, so don't worry.

A few days later, she was writing:

> The widower has been invisible since morning so my heart is cold with longing. I have been looking at the possibility from all sides—but there are so many objections to falling in love with him. Not considering that I prefer Detroit and my own home to anybody's, the gent's name is so suggestive of cheese that we call him Mr. Scent.... Then he is a Norwegian, I think, and for a very small consideration I object to him on general principles. So even with all his cash I can't find it in my heart to bother with him.

Evangeline's reference to the gent's "cash" reflects the prevalent Little Falls gossip to the effect that C.A. was one of the richest men in town—he was said to be worth a quarter of a million dollars. Having assured her mother that she couldn't find it in her heart to bother with him, the next day Evangeline continued to debate herself:

> Your letters are the most fun that I have up here except an occasional smile from the widower. Guess I must be falling in love with him, for he is the chief thing I have to write about. Yet I am

still sure that I don't want him. He is a lawyer and a bit too sharp-witted. So I'll look around a bit longer.

A week later:

Had another dandy letter from my Mamma today and in it she says (very impolitely) the "widower be hanged" or something to that effect, so I shall break the news gently—<u>he</u> walked back to school with <u>me</u> today and invited me to go with him to call on some out-of-town nabobs, the Morrels. Seeing as they asked him to do so, I accepted and sometime me and him [sic] are going. Now aren't you worried? And the worst of it is that though he is as homely as possible, I like him quite well. Now what have you to say?

Since C.A. was an extraordinarily handsome man—handsomer than any of the Lands or Lodges—Evangeline's reference to his being homely may have been intended to prepare her mother for a pleasant surprise. Mrs. Land was evidently raising objections to a possible match, and was perhaps also warning her daughter against committing any indiscretions. By November, Evangeline was firing off letters at the rate of two a day:

Wrote to you at noon and am hoping that the letter will not make you worry. You would be perfectly satisfied if you were here and could see just exactly how things are, and I am coming home in seven weeks. Please don't write me another scolding letter, because I am unhappy all day long if your letter isn't full of nice things. It seems as if I could hardly wait to get back. Just be sure that you can have your finger in all my pies and then I am sure you will not worry....

By December, she and C.A. had plainly come to an understanding; her mother would have to make the best of things:

I have asked Mr. L. to come New Year's and then bring me back here. Does this arrangement suit you? He will be very easy to entertain. He is going to Portland, Oregon, next Thursday on business and will come to Detroit from there. I am so afraid that you will not like him at first, but it won't take you long to change your mind.

# LINDBERGH ALONE

Evangeline and C.A. were married at her parents' home in Detroit in March, 1901, and they honeymooned for several weeks in California. In May, they returned to Little Falls and set about building a considerable mansion on a bluff above the Mississippi, a couple of miles south of Little Falls. C.A. had owned the property for several years—a hundred and twenty acres of gently rolling oak and pine woodland, well watered and with scattered pastures and fields. He had bought the land for its beauty, and now he meant to develop it into a country estate worthy of the position he had attained in the community; worthy, too, of his bride, who had no doubt made it clear to him, as she had to her mother, that Little Falls was no Detroit. At Evangeline's urging, they gave the property the name of Lindholm, which was an approximate Swedish abbreviation of "Lindbergh house." Grand as it was intended to be, they never referred to it as an estate; it was "the farm," though little actual farming was ever done on it, and that little—undertaken largely by young Charles, during the First World War, as a patriotic duty—was unsuccessful. Only dairy farming could be made to pay in that part of the country, and it had to be carried out on a far greater scale than the Lindbergh property permitted.

The main house was a big wooden structure, three stories high, containing thirteen rooms. It had a cavernous, stone-walled basement, a ground floor with living room, dining room, study, kitchen, and laundry, and, on the two upper floors, seven bedrooms and a billiards room. Among the outbuildings were a caretaker's cottage, a barn, and an ice-house, and paths led down to the grassy bank of the Mississippi on one side of the house and, on the other side, through tall pines and oaks to Pike Creek. While the house was under construction that summer, C.A. and Evangeline roughed it in a temporary cabin a few yards away. She was pregnant by then and proud of herself; this was the happiest time that she and C.A. were ever to know together and, characteristically, they left no record of it. As their son was to note many years later, in his <u>Wartime Journals</u>, the busiest and most interesting days of our lives often go unremarked, simply because they <u>are</u> the

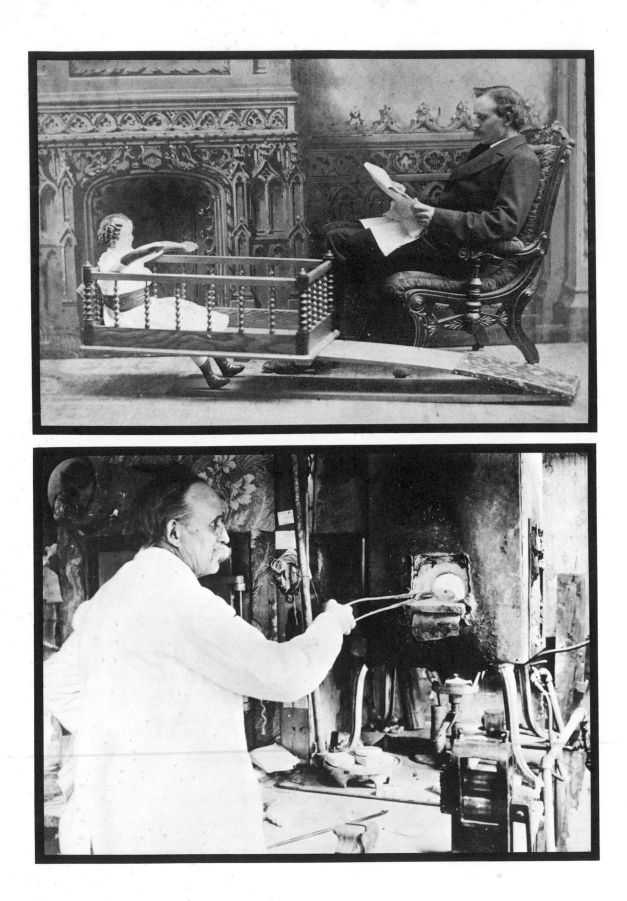

The combined residence-office-laboratory of Charles's grandfather Dr. Charles Land.

(Opposite page, top) One of Dr. Land's many inventions—a cradle in which an infant could amuse itself by bouncing up and down, or could be bounced up and down by somebody applying pressure to the carpeted end of the plank. This is the photograph that Dr. Land submitted along with his application for a patent, which was granted. (Opposite page, bottom) Dr. Land firing some false teeth.

The big house at Little Falls, begun when C.A. and Evangeline had just returned from their honeymoon, in 1901, and destroyed by fire in 1905.

Charles sets off a charge in a toy bronze cannon that his grandfather Land cast for him.

busiest and most interesting; one is often too tired at the close of such days to trouble with setting down an account of them.

Not for a moment did Evangeline consider having her baby in Little Falls; that event was to be saved as a special treat for the family in Detroit. She would be able to have the baby in her parents' house and one of her doctor-uncles would be reassuringly on hand to deliver it. She moved to Detroit well in advance of the predicted date of birth and the baby was born without difficulty on February 4, 1902. The one thing about him that everyone commented on was the length of his feet, which hinted that he would grow into an exceptionally tall man. (His father and paternal grandfather were both five feet, eleven inches tall; his mother and his grandfather Land were short. Lindbergh in his twenties stood six feet, two and a half inches tall—by far the tallest Land or Lindbergh that ever was.) The baby was named Charles Augustus, Jr., without discussion; luckily, his first name served to pay homage to Grandfather Land and Uncle Charles Land as well as to C.A.

After a further stay of several weeks in Detroit, Evangeline and Charles, Jr., returned to Little Falls and took up residence in Lindholm. With them in the house were Lillian and Eva Lindbergh, C.A.'s two daughters by his first wife. Lillian was fourteen and Eva was nine; up to then, they had been staying with one or another of their many Lindbergh relatives. They were glad to be back with their father and for a time, at least, they were glad to be with their young and pretty stepmother. Soon it became apparent that Evangeline knew little about bringing up children, to say nothing of step-children too close to her in age ever to have been her own. They were their father's daughters, stalwart and undemonstrative, and Evangeline was naturally tempted to devote most of her time and attention to little Charles. Meanwhile, the father took care to be out in the world, attending to his career. Although he had few close friends, he had a host of admirers, and he was beginning to be spoken of as a man who should run for Congress—his blunt and honest kind, championing farmers and small businessmen over Eastern bankers and other parasites, was much needed in Washington.

One of little Charles's earliest memories was of the fire that destroyed Lindholm. It happened on an August day in 1905; he was playing with his father in the parlor when he was suddenly thrust into his nurse's arms and she was ordered to carry him out of the house. She ran with him all the way to the barn—a distance of several hundred yards—in order to keep him from watching the house go up in flames. He tells the story in <u>The Spirit of St. Louis</u>, as one of the most significant of his memories:

"CHARLES!"

I hardly hear my nurse's voice above my heartbeat.

I've slipped away from her guard to stare fearfully around the gray barn's corner.

"CHARLES, COME BACK!"

A huge column of smoke is rising from our house, spreading out, and blackening the sky. Then that's what the shouts and noise all meant. That's why I was jerked away from my play so roughly and rushed down the kitchen steps. Our house is burning down!

"CHARLES!"

A hand grasps my arm and pulls me behind the barn. "Charles, you <u>mustn't</u> watch!" My nurse is excited. She thinks it's too terrible for me to see. Where is my father—my mother—what will happen to my toys?

The next day, he and his mother stand looking over the ruins of the house. Smoke still rises out of the blackened basement. His mother says, "Father will build us a new house," but somehow the child knows better—"my toys, and the big stairs, and my room above the river, are gone forever." For something has happened not only to the house but to his parents' marriage; the new house is only half the size of the old, and there is an air of makeshift about it. It is intended to be only a summer house. It is not to give parties in, not to raise a big family in. It may be that Evangeline and C.A. will go on loving each other but they are no longer in love. And the child knows.

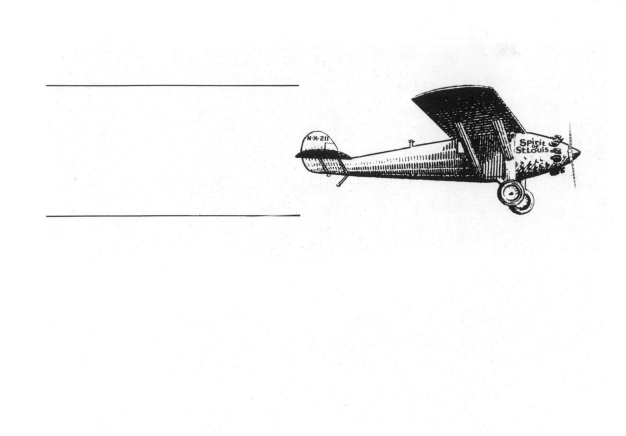

Given that they were estranged, the Lindberghs behaved with admirable discretion in regard to their child. The likelihood is that their estrangement began as early as the third or fourth year of their marriage—a marriage that was to last in name, with increasing coolness and distance, for twenty-three years—and from the start they appear to have taken care to quarrel as little as possible in front of Charles. Under the circumstances, it was fortunate that C.A. was temperamentally incapable of displays of emotion.

Like his father before him and, to a lesser degree, his son after him, C.A. was a stoic; there was scarcely any test of mental or physical anguish that he could not meet and pass without apparent distress. His failure to display the grief he undoubtedly felt over the death of his beloved first wife was much commented on in Little Falls—a community that, though not given to open emotion, thought that it knew what was appropriate on such occasions. Decades later, C.A. underwent an experience similar to that of August Lindbergh and the amputation of his arm. In his book The Hero, Kenneth S. Davis repeats a story first told a few years after the event by Lynn and Dora Haines:

> In early 1917 . . . [C.A.] asked his friend Lynn Haines to come with him to the hospital where, he said, the doctors were to perform a "little operation" on him. Actually, it was a major abdominal operation, and he endured it without anesthetic. During the hour and more that the ordeal lasted, he calmly discussed international banking and the Federal Reserve System with his friend—and Haines's wife, Dora, later recorded that C.A. "never gritted his teeth, nor even gripped Mr. Haines's hand, except for a few seconds when the surgeon's knife pierced the abdominal cavity." Afterward "he apologized for having subjected Mr. Haines to an unpleasant experience."

"An unpleasant experience"—one might well say so, and not only in respect to poor Mr. Haines but also in respect to C.A. himself. What lies behind this peculiar episode? As far as the record shows, C.A. had a normal heart and unusual stamina, and there could have been hardly any risk involved in his taking anaesthetics. He appears to have chosen to refuse them as a matter of principle, and one is tempted to imagine his having done so in emulation of his father, but the two cases have little in common: old August responded with superb courage to being operated on without anaesthetics simply because none were available. Did C.A. respond with superb courage simply because he wished to do so?

If that was the reason, then we are drawn to further speculation, for to bear pain without flinching—especially when the pain is one that can be avoided—is far more often the sign of a neurotic personality than of a healthy one. It is, indeed, so close in its nature to the act of inflicting pain that we have learned to hesitate before praising it. C.A. never wittingly inflicted physical pain upon anyone—he was even against corporal punishment for children at a time when it was an almost universal practice—but it is plain that he courted it for himself. If was remembered of him in Little Falls that he was out duckhunting with a group of men on a particularly cold fall day. They brought down a number of ducks, which fell into a lake so icy that none of the hounds accompanying the hunters dared venture into the water. Lindbergh immediately stripped off his clothes, swam out, and retrieved the birds. On another occasion, in the course of a bitter political campaign, the car in which he was being driven away from a rally was fired upon at murderously close range. The driver quite naturally increased his speed, and Lindbergh remonstrated with him. "Don't go too fast," he said. "They'll think we're afraid of them." Plainly, in Lindbergh's scale of values death was to be preferred even to the appearance of cowardice. Many years later, his son far out over the Atlantic kept repeating to himself that the worst he had to look forward to was death or failure, death or failure, death or failure; unlike most of the rest of us, he did not hesitate to put death first, as the less shameful alternative.

Pain was welcome to C.A. and so was danger, with its hidden or open threat of pain. If this reflected a morbid strain in him, with sorry consequences in his private life, it also led to heroic consequences in his public life. He served several terms in Congress and never once stooped to demagoguery to

C.A. campaigning.

Grandmother Land
on the sleeping porch with Dingo.

achieve his goals. He worked hard for his constituents and accepted no informal compensation under the table. He attacked
the Catholic Church because he believed in the separation of
church and state and was severely rebuked and repudiated by
the voters for this then very risky stand. He opposed America's
entry into the First World War and was branded a traitor for
doing so. Most of the personal fortune that he had accumulated in his youth he used up defending the cause of the agrar-
ian West against the financial East. Alone and lonely and
growing old, he surrendered none of his unpopular con-
victions. The least romantic-seeming of men (as well as the
least eloquent: his political speeches often lasted for hours and
bored everyone who heard them), he nevertheless died like a
Cyrano, with gallantry, surrounded by the ghosts of innumerable enemies, whom he implacably defied.

Charles, Jr., was his only son, and almost from Charles's
birth C.A. taught him to face pain and danger as he did, with a
readiness—perhaps an eagerness—that many people regarded
as unnatural. Although he was middle-aged when Charles was
born, C.A. was in excellent physical condition. He was proud
of his sturdy, tireless body and its skills, and he was able to be a
close companion to the boy. He taught him how to fish and
hunt and hike and make fires and pitch tents and paddle a
canoe. As Charles was to write many years later, when he was
himself middle-aged, "He'd let me walk behind him with a
loaded gun at seven, use an axe as soon as I had strength
enough to swing it, drive his Ford car anywhere at twelve. Age
seemed to make no difference to him. My freedom was complete. All he asked for was responsibility in turn."

How easy a bargain Lindbergh makes it seem! Complete
freedom at the price of responsibility was "all" that his father
asked; one would never guess that this was "all" that mankind
had been striving for in vain throughout many thousands of
years, and yet Lindbergh's tone is not superior. It has not occurred to him at the moment of writing that the bargain has
proved harder for others to carry out than it has proved for generations of Lindberghs: those tow-headed, blue-eyed children

trudging along at seven with loaded guns behind their fathers are not the first image of the father-son relationships that ordinarily springs to mind.

C.A. felt no physical shyness in his son's presence. Many fathers in those days took care to conceal their bodies from their sons and—what is still more curious—took care not to see their sons' bodies. With pagan gusto, C.A. and little Charles bathed nakedly together in the fast-flowing Mississippi or in the placid shallows of Pike Creek, a few hundred yards inland from the riverbank and the Lindbergh house. Where it passed the house, the Mississippi at the turn of the century used to be filled with rapids, which the building of a power dam downstream has since submerged. The father would often plunge into the turbulent white water of the river and swim back and forth across it—a distance of several hundred yards—with the child clinging joyously to his bare back.

Charles learned to swim one day in the usual Lindbergh fashion. Wading out from shore, he found himself unexpectedly beyond his depth and being drawn into the current. In terror, he looked to his father for help and he saw that he was still on the shore and laughing at his son's plight. The son began frantically to paddle and splash and within a few seconds had discovered that he was capable of remaining afloat. In describing this episode, he reveals no hint of distress at his father's conduct: it is how fathers are meant to behave. "You and I can take hard knocks," the father told the boy. "We'll get along no matter what happens." And to the boy the hard knocks, when they came, were as nothing compared to the pride he felt in the man-to-man intimacy of that precious, unforgettable "we."

C.A. demanded an unusual degree of hardiness from little Charles; remarkably, Charles's mother made no objection. Whatever else the parents may have quarreled about—and as the estrangement persisted, it became convenient, as in most estrangements, to let money be the chief topic of discussion, since topics more important than money were less easy to broach—they never quarreled about how to raise their son. As a mother, Evangeline may often have been heartsick at the risks she saw Charles being encouraged to take, but she held her tongue. Bravely, she let Charles be brave. With the father so often away, she took special pains to let Charles—at nine or ten!—assume the role of master of the house. As the father trusted him in the woods and fields, so the mother trusted him in his judgment of domestic matters. She paid no more attention to his age than the father did: he was a fellow–human being, strong of body and with a lively mind. She and Charles admired each other. They shared the house, and the small, daily troubles of the house, as equals.

That ready sharing of equality came more naturally to Evangeline than it would have come to most young women of her day. She was bolder in thought and deed than the young wives and mothers not only of the small town of Little Falls but also of her birthplace, the bustling and progressive industrial metropolis of Detroit. She was a member of a large, self-confident, and intellectually ambitious family, and her father, the celebrated Dr. Land, was a born iconoclast. (In photographs of him taken over seventy years ago, his eyes shine out at us with an undiminishable, merry skepticism; he looks as if he were just about to crack a good joke at the expense of some pious banality, and we think at once, leaning forward involuntarily to catch the joke, "What an amusing companion he would be!") Dr. Land read and espoused Darwin, mocked the historic pretensions of Christianity, and was impatient with the social and professional conventions of the day. Indeed, he was once dismissed from the local and state dental societies for having had the temerity to patent a number of his prosthetic devices; his colleagues implied that he was attempting to get rich by these devices, instead of putting them at the service of humanity. In fact, Dr. Land showed little aptitude for making money. He was more interested in controlling the disposition of his inventions than he was in commercially exploiting them. The Lindbergh and Land families were always alike in this: that they enjoyed making money, but that there were other things that they enjoyed still more. So it was with Charles, when his chance came; he grew rich, but not as rich as he could have been—only as rich as he needed to be in order to choose freely the life that he thought would suit him best.

Although by descent Evangeline was mostly English and Scottish, she attributed her adventurousness to her Irish grandmother and she looked for evidences of Irishness in her son Charles. She would refer, for example, to his "Irish" hair, meaning that it was unruly. The truth was that C.A. as a young man had hair almost identical to Charles's, but as the years passed Evangeline had reason to find less and less to admire in Swedes. It had been adventurous of her to go away to college, still more adventurous of her to take a teaching position in Little Falls. It had also been adventurous—at any rate, it had been hot-tempered and, therefore, in her view commendably Irish—of her to quit her job when the superintendent of the high school insisted on her teaching in a cold classroom at the top of the school building and she insisted on moving her students and her chemistry equipment downstairs to a warm one. If she had not been contemplating marriage, she would have left the town at once. As she wrote at the time to her mother, "I shall tell you one thing surely that no matter what becomes of me and my friend the lawyer, Little Falls, Minnesota, shall not see very much more of this chicken. She wants Detroit and her Mamma and Papa and Brother."

Yet Evangeline stayed and was married (and what could have been more reckless than to take as a bridegroom a near-stranger seventeen years older than she?). When the marriage deteriorated, she grew less reckless and less outspoken. She felt a sense of being unjustly imprisoned inside the marriage, and C.A. as her judge and jailer had no intention of setting her free. For the first time, he was running for Congress and a divorce would have meant, in that time and place, an immediate end to his political career. He would give her no grounds for a divorce. When she asked for a legal separation, he refused her that as well. They must remain husband and wife; it would be better for the child. Better for his career, better for his pocketbook, Evangeline protested to her mother in Detroit, and yet for all she knew to the contrary he might be right; perhaps it <u>would</u> be better for the child. She wrote that she was unworldly and ignorant; moreover, she feared the disapprobation of the

(Top) Charles and his father out hunting.

(Above) Dr. Land and Charles.

(Left) Charles in a canoe on the Mississippi. (Like so many family snapshots of those days, this is a double-exposure. To Charles's right is a second Charles.)

Charles experimenting with the family cat, Fluff, at Grandfather Land's.

Dr. Land's experimental laboratory, in which he invented new kinds of false teeth, artificial jawbones, and the like.

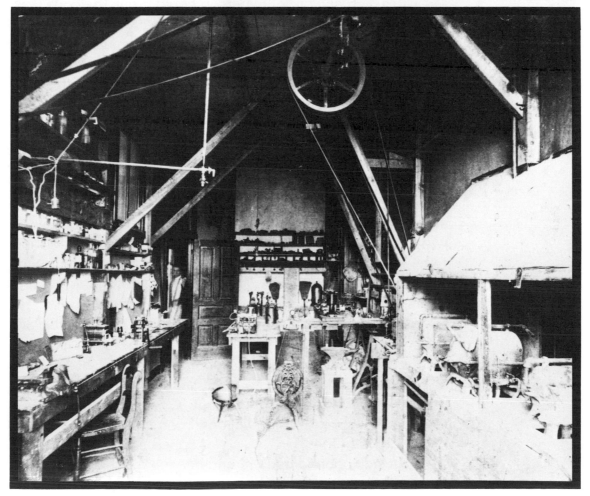

older and richer "society" women in Little Falls and so she gave way, however grudgingly, to C.A. Off he could go to Washington, D.C., to whatever glory awaited him there, and she and the boy would tag along behind him.

At about this time, she took to writing to her mother in code. The code was a simple one, in which twenty-six numerals stood for the twenty-six letters of the alphabet, and it is hard to imagine why she thought it necessary to employ it. Were her two step-daughters, by then living with them at Lindholm, spying on her and perhaps opening her mail in their father's behalf? Unlikely, and it was still more unlikely that she believed that her letters were being opened by some unknown confederate of C.A.'s at the post office in Little Falls. Besides, the difficulty of writing in code had to be measured against the ease with which any ordinary person could break the code. It is possible that she wrote in code not because it was necessary to do so but because it was emotionally gratifying; it was always the worst things to be said about C.A. that she transferred into code, intensifying them and making them serve by their secrecy as an added bond between her mother and her. The two women were very close and, unlike many married mothers and daughters, they grew closer with the years.

Much of a letter from Evangeline to her mother would be written in the conventional fashion; here she recounts an anecdote about Charles at the age of seven: "I told him the other day that there are two kinds of men, good and bad, and went on to tell him why he must be one of the good sort. He finished me by saying, 'No, there are three kinds of men—good, bad, and the in-between kind who lie to get what they want.'" A few days later, she is writing in code to her mother about C.A.: "He sent me a check for $150 and does not mention L. [Lillian] or E. [Eva]....It has been all I could do to keep from going....The gentleman is as slippery as an eel." Some time later, writing from Washington and again in code, she says: "The other day I was terribly put out. C.A. came up Wednesday morning—took C. for a walk and came in. Charles began punching and bothering C.A., so I stopped him, but said, 'You see, C.A., he's cooped up here and needs an outlet for surplus energy.' C.A. said, 'Get up on a chair, Charles, and I'll fight you.' Charles did and let out with his foot. Evidently he hit a sore place, for C.A. grabbed him by both arms, whirled him around, and called him a fool. I simply opened the door and said, 'C.A., it is time for you to go.'"

We catch few glimpses of how the child behaved in the course of the long and increasingly bitter détente. He was handed back and forth between the parents, loving them both and looking up to them both and striving not to take sides. On one occasion, Evangeline writes of a visit by C.A., in the course of which she complained of some rudeness that she had suffered from a stranger the day before and C.A. said "in a very sarcastic way that it was 'better not to talk at all when such things happen,' that 'feeling sore over it was only punishing myself,' and that 'nothing could ever punish him mentally, as he would not allow it to.' I told him a few things myself and when we were through I asked the boy if he thought it quarreling when his father said things like that to answer them and the boy said, 'No, you answered him just right, I don't see what makes Father act so.'"

The three remarks by C.A., as quoted by Evangeline, are worth noting in one respect at least—that, the tone of sarcasm aside, they might have been uttered by Charles Lindbergh himself, some forty years after the time that his father uttered them. What a child silently apprehends and then weaves into the fabric of the person he will become! Lindbergh was always to speak of his childhood as idyllic, and it is plain that he achieved that view of it in part by a suppression of the many ugly currents that flowed across it and in part by his mother's taking care to conceal from him far more than she ever told. The passionate "Irish" impulsiveness of her girlhood and young womanhood turned rancorous, and by an act of remarkable discipline she kept most of her rancor to herself. In only one way—and a way thoroughly unexpected—did she appear to punish the child indirectly for her unhappiness, and that was in regard to his schooling.

Not until he was in his twenties did Lindbergh ever complete a school term. He was constantly being transferred from school to school, in accordance with his parents' needs and not his own. He would be now in Little Falls, now in Detroit or Washington, and sometimes he would be in temporary residence in some such unexpected place as Redondo Beach, where he and his mother spent a few months in 1916, at the conclusion of a difficult and exhausting motor trip from Minnesota to California. Little Falls was where he liked best to be, but even there he found school unsympathetic; without the assurance that his classmates felt as they moved in an orderly fashion from term to term and from year to year towards graduation, naturally he did less well in his studies than his obvious intelligence argued that he ought to be able to do. In Little Falls he had the enjoyment of his beloved woods and fields and streams and the great river itself, and in the course of his and his mother's often protracted visits to Detroit, he had the companionship of his lively little grandfather to look forward to—they would tinker together in the grandfather's smoky laboratory, or take jaunts out into the nearby countryside—but in Washington he not only disliked going to school, he disliked the city itself. Living in cramped quarters in a small apartment on an ordinary city street, a country-bred boy could find hardly any enterprise worth undertaking—no dams to build; no suspension bridges of barbed wire and rough planking to hang in air from bank to bank of Pike Creek.

Not that he wasn't aware of the importance to his father of being a Congressman and not that he didn't enjoy having a Congressman for a father—C.A. was reckoned a distinguished man on the Hill and his little blond son was often to be seen scooting around the Capitol grounds on roller-skates or accompanying his father to the House chamber. Once, when he was thirteen, he went with C.A. to the White House, to meet President Wilson. The President shook hands with Charles and asked him civilly how he was and Charles replied with equal civility, "Very well, thank you." That evening, he informed his mother that he had not been unduly excited by the encounter; the President, after all, was a man like any other. On landing in Paris and being feted by innumerable presidents, prime min-

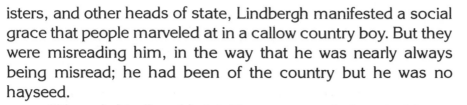

isters, and other heads of state, Lindbergh manifested a social grace that people marveled at in a callow country boy. But they were misreading him, in the way that he was nearly always being misread; he had been of the country but he was no hayseed.

Although Lindbergh's intelligence was obvious to his parents and teachers, it was not obvious to him. Doing badly in school is often the occasion for doing worse; a downward spiral of grades is hard to reverse when one's confidence is steadily spinning downward as well. Lindbergh once told his wife that, having been shuttled back and forth among a dozen schools throughout his youth, he reached a point where he couldn't be sure whether he possessed any real intelligence at all; injurious as it was to his pride, on the evidence of his grades it appeared that he must be "dumber" than most of his by no means exceptionally gifted classmates.

His failure as a student was painful enough; still more painful was his failure to become a member of any group. He was an outsider, and not only—not even mostly—by choice. Temperamentally, as the son of those practiced loners C.A. and Evangeline, and as a grandson of August Lindbergh and Charles Land, who were also loners, young Lindbergh might have been expected to embody a certain austere stand-offishness. The isolation that he actually experienced was something less intentional than that and far grimmer. Any boy who starts a school term late is probably doomed to find himself at the bottom of the traditional school pecking order. That was often Lindbergh's situation and he made matters all the more awkward for himself by a laconic manner and a seeming lack of concern for how he was treated. He didn't seek attention by kowtowing to others, he didn't volunteer answers in class, and for all his good looks and enviable height he didn't try to establish friendships with girls. He rarely attempted any of the competitive sports—baseball, football, basketball—that form the foundation of group activities in school and that, if one doesn't participate in them, brand one as something of a pariah. In those days, the only extracurricular activity that was open to both girls and boys was dancing, and Lindbergh never learned to dance.

It was only at college, indeed, that Lindbergh engaged in a competitive team activity for the first and last time; he became a member of the ROTC rifle team at the University of Wisconsin. But to be a crack shot (which Lindbergh assuredly was: in official competitions, he often scored fifty bull's-eyes in succession) is not really to be a member of a team; in a sense, it enjoins upon one the opposite of team play, since one can neither receive help from teammates nor offer it to them. The more thoroughly one is cut off from everything except one's rifle and the distant target, the better one can perform. Nothing could sum up more poignantly the loneliness of the types of excellence that Lindbergh pursued than this: that they were always activities which required him to compete not against others but against himself. The flight to Paris was only the most extreme example of this loneliness.

In the light of how little interest Charles had in his studies, it was just as well that a quirk of history insured his graduation from high school. The United States entered the World War in 1917 and as a part of the national effort to raise more food it was decreed throughout Minnesota that any boy who worked full time on a farm would be given credit for having passed a successful year in school. Charles was delighted by this arrangement. Much of his senior year he spent turning the hitherto "pretend" farm of Lindholm into a real one. He persuaded his father to stock the place with cattle, hogs, and poultry, to buy a tractor and other gear, and to undertake the building of a new barn and silo. It was as an authentic dairyman and farmer that Charles graduated with the class of 1918 from the Little Falls High School. He was only sixteen, but he could keep as long hours as any man. At that moment, he was convinced that he had seen the last of mere book-learning; he would make his way in the world as his Swedish forebears had done, by cultivating the land.

As far as one can tell, both parents were content with Charles's decision, and it is curious that they should have been. C.A. had struggled hard to lift himself up out of the ruck of manual labor on his father's farm (as his father before him had done, only to be thrust back down again by financial reverses and political scandal), and the means of C.A.'s deliverance had been education. He as a lawyer and Evangeline as a schoolteacher were both conspicuous embodiments of the advantage of going to college and yet between them they contrived a life for their son that rendered the prospect of a college education for him improbable.

When they denied Charles the opportunity to pursue an ordinary school career, with the comrades and shared experiences that furnish the usual accompaniment to such a career, did they do so out of an innocent selfishness, or were they to some degree unconsciously using Charles as a means of punishing each other through him? Was C.A. too busy and too often absent from home to see, or did he see and choose to ignore, the consequences of Evangeline's plucking Charles out of school to go on visits here and there, little by little making

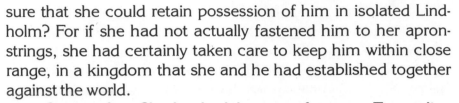

sure that she could retain possession of him in isolated Lindholm? For if she had not actually fastened him to her apronstrings, she had certainly taken care to keep him within close range, in a kingdom that she and he had established together against the world.

Once, after Charles had become famous, Evangeline was accused in print of having considered herself so superior socially to her neighbors in Little Falls that she had refused to let Charles play with their children. Lindbergh protested in private on her behalf that, on the contrary, she had sometimes paid the neighbors' children small sums for the very purpose of making sure that he had someone to play with. But the defense is more bewildering than the accusation, for why should any such payment have been necessary? How had it come about that this appealing boy had no close friends with whom to share his hours? With a charm that was one day to be responded to instantly throughout the world, how did he manage to pass almost unnoticed among his generation of boys and girls in Little Falls? When reporters descended upon the town in the summer of 1927, seeking every scrap of information about Lindbergh's past, few of the townspeople could remember much of anything about him, except that he had a mechanical bent, liked to ride a motorcylce, and never dated. Little as she may have been aware of it, Evangeline's need to sequester and dominate her son was very strong. Charles was hers, and the evidence is that for twenty-seven years no other woman came within touching distance of him. Few mothers have held the absolute fealty of their sons for so long.

Throughout the course of the war, Charles worked the farm with some measure of success, but by 1919, when the war was over, farm prices began to fall and it was clear that no matter how stubbornly he and his hired man might labor to make a profit, Lindholm was too small to compete against the large-scale dairy farms in the neighborhood. What Charles had hoped would be the beginning of a career more congenial to him than school turned out to be a failure even greater than his failure at school. Although the circumstances that had caused him to fail were obviously beyond his control, the blow must have been a bitter one; he had done his best and his best had not sufficed.

In 1969, at the urging of his friend Russell W. Fridley, Director of the Minnesota Historical Society, Lindbergh wrote a letter setting down his recollection of early days at Lindholm. The house and land had long been a part of the Charles A. Lindbergh State Park, given to the state of Minnesota by members of the Lindbergh family in the early nineteen-thirties, as a memorial to the Congressman. Lindbergh began the letter with characteristic matter-of-factness:

Dear Russell:
I find myself with the unusual experience of a completely free day! I expected to fly to northeastern Luzon, in a light plane I have rented, for about a week's visit with some of the "primitive" Philippine tribes, but my take-off from Manila has been postponed until tomorrow morning.

Remembering my promise to write about some of the background of Lindbergh State Park, I shall start now. I don't know when this letter will be finished, or from where it will be mailed.

As it turned out, the letter amounted to eighty-five manuscript pages, written in half a dozen places, including a grass hut in Luzon ("I write in pencil because it is so humid that the paper blots with ink...") and the air above the North Atlantic. The letter turned out to be interesting enough for Fridley to ask if the Society might publish it as a book. Lindbergh consented, and it came out in 1972 under the title Boyhood on the Upper Mississippi. In the course of the letter, Lindbergh speaks of his abandonment of the farm as being "rather" heartbreaking—under the circumstances, a curious adverb: surely a thing is either heartbreaking or it is not? But perhaps for Lindbergh "heartbreaking" was a word too strong to leave unmodified.

In 1919 I turned the farm over to tenants again [there had been tenants on the farm at an earlier period] in preparation for going away to college. It was a difficult and rather heart-breaking procedure, giving up the stock and machinery and seeing my methods and hopes give way to the methods and hopes of others.... I spent a good deal of time selecting the col-

On his Excelsior motorcycle.

On his motrocycle journeys throughout the West and South, Lindbergh often slept by the side of the road at night. Here, the Excelsior has been dismantled for repairs.

At the University of Wisconsin.

lege I wanted to enter and finally chose the University of Wisconsin—probably more because of its nearby lakes than because of its high engineering standards. Then, as now, I could not be happy living long away from water. In the fall of 1920 I rode my Excelsior motorcycle from the farm to Madison, Wisconsin, and entered the college of mechanical engineering. That ended all my close contacts with our farm.

His parents had been pleased by his decision to take a chance on going to college. Because of his marked mechanical aptitude, they agreed that he should seek a degree in mechanical engineering; with a degree in hand, they were sure that there would be many choices of employment open to him. Best of all from Evangeline's point of view was the fact that she wouldn't be losing him. On the contrary, she moved with Charles to Madison, rented a flat for them on the third floor of an old house near the university, and secured a position for herself as a teacher of science in a local junior high. She would never again live at Lindholm, never again be in C.A.'s shadow; her long domestic imprisonment was ended and she looked forward not only to the freedom she would share with Charles but also to the resumption of her professional career.

The money Evangeline earned was more than a pleasing proof of independence. It was necessary, because she and Charles were receiving less and less financial help from C.A. He was out of office and had lost a great deal of money in three unsuccessful political campaigns, in ill-timed real-estate deals, and in the financing of a radical magazine, Lindbergh's National Farmer, which, after a brave start, slowly petered out. Taxes on the farm often went unpaid, and C.A. and Evangeline bickered back and forth by mail as to whether Charles's college education should be paid for by an extensive mortgaging of the property or by some other means. Evangeline invariably suspected C.A. of trying to put something over on her and would urge Charles to reason with his father.

Charles drifted through the first year of college with low grades and, to his mother's dismay, sank to still lower depths in his second year. In February, 1922, she received the following communication from Charles's adviser, who was not in so intimate an advisory position as to have mastered his young charge's first name:

Mrs. C. A. Lindbergh,
35 North Mills Street,
Madison,
Wisconsin.

My dear Madam:

The record made by Carl during the first semester is very discouraging.

Machine Design I.....................................Failure
Mathematics 52.....................................Failure
Physics 51 ............................................Incomplete
Shop 6 .................................................88
Shop 13 ...............................................88

It seems to me that Carl is quite immature and that a boy of his temperament might do better in some less technical course than engineering. In my conversation with him during the semester he seemed to agree with me on that point.

On account of the above poor record the Sophomore Adviser Committee decided on February 2 that Carl should be dropped from the University.

Yours very truly,
P. H. Hyland
Adviser

The letter arrived a few days after Charles's twentieth birthday. Probably the most unexpected news it contained was that Mr. Hyland considered "Carl" immature. To almost everyone else who had ever encountered him, Charles's most striking aspect had been the naturalness with which he shouldered adult responsibilities. In appearance he remained uncannily boyish-looking well into middle age, but except for his weakness for horseplay and practical jokes there was little that was boyish in his character. He had been playing a man's role at Lindholm from the age of ten or twelve, he had driven his mother and uncle across country by car at the age of fourteen, at fifteen and sixteen he had traveled alone by motorcycle for thousands of miles throughout the West and South and had been running a farm....Immature! His academic failure was humiliating enough, but the accusation of immaturity must have been the most grievous blow of all.

Those winter weeks of 1922 were surely the nadir of Lindbergh's life. History as the product of hindsight has the advantage of perceiving the amount of good and evil fortune that befalls a man in the course of an entire lifetime; knowing, as the man himself cannot, that certain rewards or punishments are in store for him, history gives a balance to his life that often bears little relationship to how that life has been experienced. Especially does history tend to underestimate the degree of suffering that the young feel when they fail. For at the time, the failure is total and looks as if it might be everlasting. Lindbergh at twenty, at the end of a long succession of failures, had no way of foreseeing that in five years he would be the best-known and most admired person on the face of the earth.

I n the first half of my sophomore year I left college to learn to fly." Determined truth-teller though he was, in writing The Spirit of St. Louis some twenty-five years after the event Lindbergh was able to bring himself to say only that he had left college, not that he had been dismissed from it. He also remembered his departure from college as being earlier than it was, perhaps in order to reenforce, by a substantial gap in time, his belief that the decision had been his and not that of the authorities. One is interested to note these trifling, telltale readjustments of the past, but it is the end of the quoted sentence that is of importance, for from the moment that he undertook to learn to fly, Lindbergh's life changed utterly. With one enormous exception—his attempt, at first singly and then in conjunction with the America First Committee, to keep the United States from entering the Second World War—he was never to know failure again; whatever he sought to achieve, he achieved.

The transformation that flight worked in Lindbergh's life was so profound that it has the aspect of a fairy tale. To the non-flier, the very act of flying contains a large measure of the magical, and it was as if Lindbergh in taking to the air had immediately acquired some preternatural capacity for self-fulfillment that ordinary mortals lacked. It was a capacity that was bound to put him at a distance from most of his contemporaries (the exceptions would include his fellow-fliers) and, even before the Paris adventure, would cause him to be placed in the category of hero. Lindbergh was distressed and irritated whenever he was described by that term; he protested in vain that he didn't feel like a hero, and to him the word evidently had a mushy, journalistic sound, at the opposite pole from— but no more accurate than—the detested "Lucky Lindy." Still, when he was a gypsy flier barnstorming around the West in 1922 and 1923, wing-walking and giving exhibition parachute jumps, and when, some time later, on several occasions he had to bail out of a plane in order to save his life, his coolness in the face of danger struck others as having the indisputable stamp of the heroic upon it. For the hero is not merely brave in times of grave peril—he is calm, he is perhaps even expectant.

The moment of the encounter between life and death exhilarates him; it is the moment for which all the days of his life have been preparing him.

Because Lindbergh's career was to be so intimately linked to flight, he seems in retrospect to have approached it comparatively late—he went up in a plane for the first time in April, 1922, and he soloed for the first time in April of the following year, in a reconditioned wartime Jenny that he had purchased only a few minutes before. There were reasons enough for his apparent tardiness. For one thing, few planes ever landed in Little Falls; when a barnstormer did come by, offering five-dollar rides to the local inhabitants, the Lindberghs felt that they had better things to spend their hard-earned money on. For another thing, both Evangeline and C.A. were skeptical of the feasibility of flying. Unlike their son, neither of them had the slightest bent for mechanics; they had mastered with difficulty the art of driving a car and they could not begin to take in the implausible novelty of heavier-than-air machines. When Charles first spoke to them about the possibility that, on graduating from high school, he might try to earn a living as an aviator, they shook their heads in disapproval. C.A. put it to him bluntly: flying was dangerous and he was their only son; they couldn't afford to lose him. Moreover (though they refrained from using this crass argument with him), the world of aviation was without prestige. It was not a serious occupation, like Evangeline's teaching or C.A.'s practice of law. By all accounts, fliers were a reckless lot of harum-scarum misfits; to join their ranks would be a step down socially and in every other way for their handsome, promising son.

Thus it came about that the adolescent Lindbergh day-dreamed for years about flying without ever experiencing it. Plainly it stood in his daydreams for two precious ideals, which he came to believe in at no telling how early an age and which he cherished with increasing ardor throughout a long lifetime: the freedom to move at will from one set of circumstances to another and the exercise of total control within that freedom. Until he had made his way into the air, he would have to realize those ideals in a diminished fashion by earthbound journeys.

# LINDBERGH ALONE

To that end, he purchased from the hardware store in Little Falls a two-cylinder Excelsior motorcycle, with which he set about exploring first the adjacent countryside and then much of the country at large, on one occasion traveling as far south as Florida. Travel had served as a consolation to his mother in the years of her failed marriage and young Charles had nearly always been her eager and uncomplaining companion. As he grew up, he came to enjoy traveling alone, riding his motorcycle hour after hour over great distances and, as usual, pitting himself against challenges of nature that were both exterior and interior—cold and heat and darkness and intense sunlight outside his body, fatigue and miscalculation and a threatened loss of confidence within it.

People in Little Falls recollected in after years that Lindbergh on his motorcycle had dashed at a terrifying rate along the roads and pathways of the town, but Lindbergh always impatiently denied that this had been the case. As late as the nineteen-sixties, he picked up one of the earliest of the biographies that had been written about him—Charles Lindbergh, His Life, by Van Emery and Tracy, published in the fall of 1927—and annotated some of its many errors. The book had belonged to his mother and as he riffled through its pages he encountered a souvenir. "What chords are pulled," he wrote, "to find a four-leaf clover pressed between these pages, obviously placed there by my mother, probably more than forty years ago." On page thirty-six of the book, he came on a vivid and inaccurate description of his high-speed motorcycling. "I seldom rode my motorcycle at top speed," he noted in correction. "In fact top speed would have been impossible on any of the roads around Little Falls. I was much more interested in developing my riding skill at lower speeds—in negotiating difficult roads, in banking on turns with different surface conditions, etc. To me, the primary value of my motorcycle was for cheap and effective transportation. I loved riding it; but high speed was secondary. I liked the mechanical perfection of the motorcycle . . . and took pride in the skill I developed in riding it. I liked the feel of its power, and its response to my control. Eventually, it seemed like an extension of my own body."

Lindbergh with "Bud" Gurney, at Lincoln, Nebraska, where they both learned to fly.

H. J. Lynch, with whom Lindbergh barnstormed throughout the West.

His failure at the university made it possible for him to announce to his parents what they perhaps already knew—that whether they liked it or not, he had made up his mind to fly. The occasion on which he broke the news to his mother is described in The Spirit of St. Louis, in one of the artful flash-backs by which, in the course of a seemingly straightforward chronological account of the thirty-three and a half hours of the Atlantic flight, he recounts what he believes to be most of the salient episodes of the first twenty-five years of his life. In the ninth hour of the flight, he is thinking of the people who will be reassured if he turns aside from his projected Great Circle route to fly over the little port of St. John's, Newfoundland, dips his wings in salute, and thus makes sure that his progress up to that point will be reported to the world. Reported, that is, to his financial backers in St. Louis, to the men in San Diego who built the plane, and to Evangeline:

> My mother, teaching school in Detroit—she's probably been at her laboratory desk all day, wondering and worrying, and trying unsuccessfully, with chemistry experiments, to curtain off in her mind a pilot and his plane. How well I remember the expression on her face that winter evening, five and a half years ago, when I told her I wanted to leave college and learn to fly. I was so anxious to get into aviation that I scarcely realized what parting meant to her. "All right," she said. "If you really want to fly, that's what you should do." "You must go," she told me later. "You must lead your own life. I mustn't hold you back. Only I can't see the time when we'll be together much again." Her prophecy came true. Hundreds of letters and packages have gone back and forth between us, but I haven't been home for more than a few days at a stretch since then. But we went barn-storming together in southern Minnesota in the summer; and she's flown back and forth between Chicago and St. Louis with me on the mail route, riding on the sacks. I know what a message of my welfare would mean to her tonight.

Brave words for Evangeline to speak, because to her they were a kind of death sentence: "I can't see the time when we'll be together much again." She gave up her job in Madison and returned to Detroit, where she would be teaching chemistry in Cass Technical High School until her retirement in 1942. The "hundreds" of letters that Lindbergh mentions must have been more like thousands; Evangeline had always been an industrious correspondent and as soon as Charles went off to fly she began to pepper him with letters. When he gave up barnstorming and enrolled in the Army Air Service, his fellow-cadets at Brooks Field and Kelly Field assumed from the volume of mail he received that an infatuated girl friend was in feverish pursuit of him. He begged his mother to spare him embarrassment by writing to him less often. She replied that she had a solution to the problem: she would address envelopes to him in a number of different hands. There! she said, in effect—now they will envy you because they will think that you have a lot of girl friends, and it will really be only me. There was a coquetry in the suggestion, and there was sometimes a coquetry in the letters, especially when she would hint at the approach and subsequent dismissal of unidentified admirers. Meanwhile, the bulky envelopes, addressed in a variety of styles, kept on arriving. In reply to one of them, Charles wrote in a teasing vein:

Dear M.

Have not heard from you in three days. What's the matter. The other day the landlady said that my girl must have an awful case & handed me one of your letters.

And later he wrote, not for the last time:

... You shouldn't worry if you don't get a letter every other day as one is liable to get lost in the mail and besides I feel best when busy and write least. Write most when I haven't anything to do and consequently extremely melancholy. (Wonder if that will get by.)

Still later:

I wrote you on the 9th and this makes an average of one letter every two days. I don't know how long I can keep this up but I will attempt to be more punctilious in the future. (I think that's spelled right if there is such a word) (Hope you have to look it up and can't find it.)

Luckily for Charles, Evangeline was an entertaining cor-

On a combined holiday and barnstorming trip with Leon Klink. Klink stands in the right foreground while Lindbergh fills the tank with gas.

respondent. She reported the latest jokes that were circulating in school and she ticked off with accuracy the idiosyncrasies of her students and colleagues. There was a sufficient openness between them for her to be slangily robust in her language and for Charles, on his part, to be able to tell her an anecdote about a drunk who took off with him on a five-dollar ride and who kept trying to climb out of the cockpit in flight, bawling at the top of his lungs, "I have to take a piss!" And as the months and years passed, Evangeline kept him appraised of the family news, much of it in the nature of things concerned with the sorry changes brought about by death.

Charles's grandmother Land had died in Little Falls in 1919, of cancer, after months of devoted nursing by Evangeline, and zestful little Grandfather Land died suddenly a couple of years later. He had been in failing health for so long, Evangeline wrote Charles, that his death came no later than he would have wished—he had never been one to outstay his welcome and he went on working hard almost to the end. When C.A. died of a tumor of the brain, in 1924, Charles was unable to attend the funeral. He had already taken a short leave from the Army Air Service School at Brooks Field in order to visit his dying father in hospital. His father recognized him, but was no longer capable of speaking; silently, they clasped hands. Evangeline risked a quarrel with her step-daughters and Lindbergh in-laws by journeying to Little Falls for the funeral. She wrote Charles of having heard from several people in town that, in spite of their long and often acrimonious separation, C.A. had gone on caring for her. She was touched and grateful; there had been more to their marriage than she had dared to believe. In Charles's behalf, she bent over C.A.'s open coffin and placed a kiss on his forehead.

Soon there were vexing questions to be answered about C.A.'s estate. Evangeline and Charles had been left five-ninths of the whole, while Charles's half-sisters Lillian and Eva had been left two-ninths apiece. Nothing stirs bad blood in a family more quickly than the dividing up of a sum of money, whether large or small. There wasn't much to be inherited from C.A., for the farm was heavily mortgaged and his recent Florida real-estate speculations had proved unwise, but Evangeline, Lillian, Eva, and several Little Falls lawyers all pitched into the legal fray and Charles was occasionally required to assume something more than a spectator's role. A few weeks after his father's death, he was writing to his mother from Brooks Field:

Dear M.

Have received five letters from you since Saturday. Have an exam tomorrow on a hard subject so will answer the most important parts of this letter [a letter from Evangeline datelined Hotel Vendome, May 28, 1924].

Will forward clippings to Detroit soon.

I sent two letters to you at the Vendome. They will do no harm if received by the wrong parties.

I did not answer telegram as it read "Wire if you object." I did not object. Would rather you use your judgment as you are more closely in touch with things than I.

Father requested several times to me that in case of his death his ashes be "thrown to the four winds." I have one letter to this effect written after I enlisted.

I suggested the plane [evidently as a means of disposing of the ashes] due to a suggestion Father made last summer in Minn. It is not Eva's idea.

The time and place can be decided on later.

Oddly enough, it wasn't until some ten years afterwards that Charles picked up his father's ashes and, flying above the old August Lindbergh farm in Melrose, scattered them "to the four winds." In his papers, he gives no explanation for the delay, or for preferring Melrose to Little Falls.

Two things emerge from Charles's letters of this period. One is his delight in playing practical jokes; the other is his passage from being a mediocre student to being a brilliant one. In later years, Lindbergh was exasperated by the amount of space his successive biographers devoted to his bent for horseplay. He was acquainted with the usual psychoanalytical interpretations of practical jokes as manifestations of immature sexuality, frustrated sexuality, and the like, and he considered all such interpretations balderdash. He admitted that he had always enjoyed playing practical jokes—even in the nineteen-

sixties he would occasionally yield to the temptation to play
some childish prank on an unsuspecting friend or relative—but
he held that they needed no explanation beyond the obvious
one of high spirits. His own tendencies aside, it was certainly a
tradition in the armed forces and among fliers to play jokes;
young men living together had to have some outlet for their
energy, and in Lindbergh's view that was not to imply that it
was only their stored-up sexual energy that was being put to
use. For though Lindbergh himself remained a virgin, many of
his comrades were licentious in the extreme, and he often
wrote candidly to his mother about the amorous escapades of
one or another of his fellow-cadets or fliers.

Lindbergh confessed to being a master of the art of
squeezing toothpaste into the open mouth of a sleeper, of toss-
ing cold water into a sleeper's face in order to waken him (a
refinement of this gesture was inserting a rubber hose in his
bed), of putting scorpions and grasshoppers between people's
sheets, and of hiding needed clothing and gear on barracks
roofs and other inaccessible places. Lindbergh once gave his
mother a long account of a prank that he had been proud to
mastermind. The letter was written to her at Columbia University, where she was taking summer courses and where she
later earned a Master of Arts degree.

One of the cadets [Lindbergh wrote] has been playing a
large number of practical jokes. Almost as many as I have, in
fact. A few days ago three skunks were seen to run into a cul-
vert in front of the barracks. We couldn't smoke them out, so
we got the fire dept. to wash them out. The entire field felt both
relief and results, especially the cadet barracks, as they are
closest to the place. Well, after the crowd dispersed, we decided
that we would get even for some of these practical jokes, so I
got this cadet's pillow, pulled off the pillow-case, and by grasp-
ing certain portions of [one of the dead kitties] by the thumb
and forefinger, it was found that a stream of liquid could be directed on the pillow.

We replaced the pillow-case on the pillow on the bed and
went to sleep. The cadet in question was out "necking" (do
they use that at Columbia?) and did not come in until midnight.
Before he did come other cadets arrived who had not been pres-

ent at the skunking. The odor from the pillow by this time had permeated the entire barracks and while some of the fellows would like to murder someone (they did not realize the entire consequences when a unanimous vote had been taken on saturating the pillow), they had no one to blame but themselves.

The cadets coming in from town all thought that the skunk was in their own bunks and spent some time discovering where it did come from. By midnight about as many men were in the barracks as were outside sleeping on the ground. About as many retained remnants of their supper as did not. When the joker finally did arrive and got near his bunk, he thought that the entire outfit had been fumigated and refused to sleep on any part of it. He slept outside that night and has just begun to use his mattress and borrowed sheets and blankets.

Two footnotes: Lindbergh was evidently so pleased with the prank that he didn't mind having to become one of the victims of its success. And it is to be remembered that sleeping out of doors, on the ground, instead of indoors, in a bed, would have been less of a hardship for Lindbergh than for most of his fellow-cadets: all his life he was in the habit of stripping the covers off a bed in a luxury hotel and fashioning a monkish pallet for himself on the floor. As for the question of whether the slang word "necking" had yet come into use at Columbia, Evangeline answered, with who knows what degree of accuracy, that it had not.

Perhaps the most complex practical joke that Lindbergh ever devised he recollected with gusto in some notes written in 1969. The notes reveal in him a welcome Rabelaisian carnality that many people, knowing him only as a public figure, would have been quick to assume he lacked. They saw him as prim, which he wasn't; he had an old-fashioned sense of the fitness of things according to time and place, though on occasion that sense of fitness collided with a boyish impulse to turn the world upside down. Lindbergh was writing these notes privately but not with the intention that they should ever be destroyed; he expected that sooner or later they would be for other people's eyes and he took care as well as relish in setting them down—a white-haired man remembering the bawdy mischief-making of his youth.

Lindbergh's second plane was a Canuck, the Canadian equivalent of a Jenny. Here Evangeline Lindbergh is togged for flight.

Lindbergh testing a Hardin parachute in Burlington, Colorado.

The Canuck was underpowered as well as rickety. Once, trying for a quick take-off from a desert in Texas, Lindbergh impaled the Canuck on a Spanish dagger plant, which ripped open the lower wing.

Lindbergh and Klink repairing the wing with crating wood, canvas, glue, nails, and chalk line.

One of the cadets in my class at Brooks Field [the notes begin] frequently patronized the brothels in San Antonio's "Spick Town." He was a huge man and he used to brag about his activities in Spick Town. He was an extraordinarily deep sleeper.

On a hot Texas weekend afternoon, he was lying naked and asleep on top of his barracks-room bunk. He lay on his back, and his penis, proportioned to his size, was standing erect and stiff. Several cadets began discussing what action it would be appropriate to take. I suggested that we paint the penis green. (I knew where some green paint and a brush were easily available.)

Our mission accomplished, the cadet remained still sleeping and still in the same condition. We then screwed a metal "eye" into the ceiling over his bunk, passed a long string through it, fashioned a lasso at one end of the string, and ran the other end out of a window. After lassoing the penis, one cadet took station outside the window and the rest of us sat on our bunks, apparently reading or talking.

When the end of the string was pulled, the cadet woke up, rose on his elbows, and stared at his green-painted penis. He had a grand sense of humor. All he said was "Je-sus CHRIST!"

This anecdote contains two clues to the nature of the incurable practical joker. The first is that when the cadets saw the sleeping cadet in erection, they immediately began discussing what action it would be appropriate to take; the idea of not taking action under the circumstances was unthinkable. The second clue is Lindbergh's admiring "He had a grand sense of humor." That is invariably the highest praise the practical joker can bestow upon one of his victims. The giant cadet was obviously entitled to leap out of bed (having removed the string) and begin assaulting his tormentors, but not at all—he had a grand sense of humor.

A practical joke that, almost half a century later, Lindbergh confessed feeling embarrassed by had as its victim his early chum "Bud" Gurney. They had met in Lincoln, Nebraska, at the flying school of which Lindbergh had proved to be the only paying student. Together they had gone up in a plane for the first time. The joke on Gurney was played some three years later, when Lindbergh was getting ready to fly the mail between St. Louis and Chicago. The third party mentioned, Phil Love, had been a fellow-cadet of Lindbergh's and had been chosen by him as one of his two assistant pilots. The Gurney joke:

> Phil Love and I were rooming together in the Brayton house, at the edge of Lambert Field. Bud Gurney had rented a room next to us, on the second floor. Love and I kept a bucket of drinking water in a corner of our kitchen. Bud came, day after day and week after week, to drink our water when he was thirsty, but he never took a turn at filling the bucket from the pump in the yard. He wasn't lazy. Actually, he was a very hard worker. He just never thought about filling that bucket. One day, I threw out the water and partly filled the bucket with kerosene.
>
> It never occurred to me that Bud would take more than a sip, if that, before he found out that it was kerosene in the bucket. Also, I knew that kerosene wasn't very harmful if taken internally, because the old Norwegian on our farm in Minnesota used to drink a small tumbler of kerosene as a cold cure.
>
> But Bud loved to eat chocolate-covered cherries, and he came into our kitchen with a mouthful of them to get a drink of water. Neither Love nor I were there at the time. Bud said afterward that he took two big gulps from the dipper before he realized that he was not drinking water!

Along with the practical jokes, how hard Lindbergh worked! He might have argued, indeed, that the practical jokes he played during this period were not merely a sign of youthful energy but also of his need, from time to time, to break the tension of an extreme intellectual effort. For from being an indifferent student in high school and a total failure at the University of Wisconsin he became, almost overnight, the star of his class in flying school—a class of one hundred and four cadets that had already passed sufficiently stringent mental and physical examinations and had been selected from a large body of applicants from coast to coast.

The hours of instruction in the air were, of course, easier for Lindbergh than for most of the other cadets at Brooks Field. He had logged over three hundred hours of flying time, while many of his fellow-cadets had never flown at all; moreover, he had made many exhibition parachute jumps and had

performed other feats of aerial derring-do that even his hard-boiled instructors at Brooks had reason to feel awestruck by. Also impressive was the fact that he had arrived at the school in his own plane—a battered and patched Canuck, one of whose wheels lacked a tire and whose fabric had been so slashed to tatters by the wind that the ground personnel at the field refused to believe that it would ever fly again. Lindbergh was able to prove otherwise. He had scores of crack-ups and forced landings and unnerving take-offs behind him, and each of them had taught him something of value. He and any plane he flew quickly became one; like his motorcycle, a plane served as an extension of the muscles of his body, responding at once to the bidding of his mind.

Although he had full confidence in his flying ability, Lindbergh was alarmed by what might befall him in the classroom at Brooks. Failure there would be every bit as calamitous as failure in the air, and he was conscious of the fact that throughout the years cadets would be "washed out" at a steady rate, with perhaps a fifth of the class managing to receive its wings upon graduation. As usual, Lindbergh looked a difficult situation in the face and sought to master it by putting it as nearly as possible under his total control. In the case of study, this meant leaving much less to chance than he had been accustomed to doing; no longer could he drift along, hoping improbably for the best. He decided, therefore, to _will_ himself into a wholly new attitude towards studying. A year before he died, he looked back in his "Autobiography of Values" upon that moment of decision, and the passage hints that he was well aware of what had already become the key principle of his life: the harder the problem, the better it was to embrace it, pushing oneself to the seeming limit and then (for one always surprised oneself at the last) beyond the limit. "I concluded," he wrote, "that the surest way of passing all seventy-plus examinations would be to strive for the highest marks I could get. I began studying as I had never studied before—evenings, weekends, sometimes in the washroom after bed check, far into the night. When I graduated in March 1925, I had the highest standing in my class."

I n a foreword to We, Ambassador Myron T. Herrick, writing from the United States Embassy in Paris, in June, 1927, pointed out the practical value of Lindbergh's flight in helping to mend the uneasy relations that then existed between the United States and France. This practical value was, however, only a fortunate by-product of what the Ambassador felt to be an authentic spiritual experience for both nations and, indeed, for the world. With heartfelt Victorian eloquence, Herrick compared Lindbergh's arrival in Paris to the French victory at the Marne, in the First World War:

> Just before the Battle of the Marne I was standing on the river embankment. A great harvest moon was rising over the city near Notre Dame. It seemed to rest on the corner of a building. The French flag was blowing steadily across its face. In the fleeting moments while this spectacle lasted, people knelt on the quay in prayer. I inquired the meaning of these prayers. The answer was that there is a prophecy centuries old that the fate of France will finally be settled upon the fields where Attila's hordes were halted and driven back, and where many battles in defense of France have been won. And pointing up the Seine to the French flag outlined across the moon, people cried: "See! the sign in Heaven! It means the victory of French arms! The prophecy is come true as of old and France is once more to be saved on those chalky fields."
>
> Now when this boy of ours dropped unheralded from the skies and circling the Eiffel Tower came to rest as gently as a bird on the field of Le Bourget, I was seized with the same premonition as those French people on the quay that August night. I felt, without knowing why, that his arrival was far more than a fine deed well accomplished, and there glowed within me the prescience of a splendor yet to come. Lo! It did come and has gone on spreading its beneficence upon two sister nations which a now conquered ocean joins.

From the Ambassador's point of view, "this boy of ours" was certainly unheralded, but to look back upon Lindbergh in the light of history is to perceive many signs of that splendor which was to come. Lindbergh was radically exceptional both in his ancestry and in his upbringing and from the moment of his enlistment in the Army Air Service he was radically successful in his career. The Robertsons having appointed him their chief air-mail pilot, he was probably earning as much money in his early twenties as any aviator in the country (and unlike most of his colleagues he was saving a large portion of his income; he was nothing if not prudent). Moreover, by the time Lindbergh was getting ready for the New York–to–Paris adventure, he had made four emergency parachute jumps, from planes that he had been forced to abandon. No other man in the country had made so many.

The first of these jumps is of lasting interest because it marked the first time that anyone had ever survived the collision of two planes in the air. Lindbergh's official report of the accident was remarkable not alone for the facts it contained but for the skill with which it was written. Eventually, the report made its way into <u>Aviation</u> magazine, and then into the New York <u>Evening World</u>, and was reprinted and used in schools as a model of unadorned narrative style. His mother, reading of the academic purpose to which his report was being put, wrote to him gleefully to say that she hoped his English professor at Wisconsin was aware of how well his once much-criticized former student was doing—better, she felt sure, than any other English student the professor had ever had.

The complete text of the report goes as follows:

Report by Cadet C.A. Lindbergh on the collision in air between S.E. 5.E. No. 50 piloted by Lt. McAllister and S.E. 5.E. No. 55 piloted by Cadet C.A. Lindbergh at about 8:50 A.M. March 6th, 1925, approximately ten miles north of Kelly Field.

A nine-ship SE-5 formation, commanded by Lieutenant Blackburn, was attacking a DH4B, flown by Lieutenant Maughan at about a 5,000 foot altitude and several hundred feet above the clouds. I was flying on the left of the top unit, Lieut. McAllister on my right, and Cadet Love leading. When we nosed down on the DH, I attacked from the left and Lieut. McAllister from the right. After Cadet Love pulled up, I continued to dive on the DH for a short time before pulling up to the left. I saw no other ship nearby. I passed above the DH and a moment later felt a slight jolt followed by a crash. My head was thrown forward against the cowling and my plane seemed to turn around and hang nearly motionless for an instant. I closed the throttle and saw an SE-5 with Lieut. McAllister in the cockpit, a

Lindbergh adjusting his parachute at Lambert Field, just before take-off on the flight that led to his second emergency parachute jump. (The first had been as a cadet in the Army Air Service.)

After bailing out, he landed in a potato patch and dislocated his shoulder.

few feet on my left. He was apparently unhurt and getting ready to jump.

Our ships were locked together with the fuselages approximately parallel. My right wing was damaged and had folded back slightly, covering the forward right-hand corner of the cockpit. Then the ships started to mill around and the wires began whistling. The right wing commenced vibrating and striking my head at the bottom of each oscillation. I removed the rubber band safetying the belt, unbuckled it, climbed out past the trailing edge of the damaged wing, and with my feet on the cowling on the right side of the cockpit, which was then in a nearly vertical position, I jumped backwards as far from the ship as possible. I had no difficulty in locating the pullring and experienced no sensation of falling. The wreckage was falling nearly straight down and for some time I fell in line with its path and only slightly to one side. Fearing the wreckage might fall on me, I did not pull the rip-cord until I dropped several hundred feet and into the clouds. During this time I had turned one-half revolution and was falling flat and face downward. The parachute functioned perfectly; almost as soon as I pulled the rip-cord the risers jerked on my shoulders, the leg straps tightened, my head went down, and the chute fully opened.

I saw Lieut. McAllister floating above me and the wrecked ships pass about 100 yards to one side, continuing to spin to the right and leaving a trail of lighter fragments along their path. I watched them until, still locked together, they crashed in the mesquite about 2000 feet below and burst into flames several seconds after impact.

Next I turned my attention to locating a landing place. I was over mesquite and drifting in the general direction of a plowed field which I reached by slipping the chute. Shortly before striking the ground, I was drifting backwards, but was able to swing around in the harness just as I landed on the side of a ditch 100 feet from the edge of the mesquite. Although the impact of landing was too great for me to remain standing, I was not injured in any way. The parachute was still held open by the wind and did not collapse until I pulled in one group of shroud lines.

During my descent I lost my goggles, a vest-pocket camera which fitted tightly in my hip pocket, and the rip-cord of the parachute.

Lieut. Maughan landed his DH in the field and took our chutes back to Kelly. Twenty minutes later Captain Guidera brot

[sic] a DH and a chute over for me and I returned to Kelly Field with him.

An hour after the crash we were flying in another nine-ship S.E.5 formation with two new S.E.5's.

What is most startling about this report, especially to the non-flier, is how little startling the episode itself appears to have been to Lindbergh. For him the air had become so nearly his natural element that an astounding accident taking place a mile up in the sky was perhaps less cause for alarm than if two automobiles had collided at high speed on the ground. Deliberately and without the least hint of panic, he began to free himself from the two plummeting, windmilling planes. There was plenty of time to do everything in an orderly manner; having taken care to make a big jump backwards, away from all that bristling wreckage, he then took care to fall free for hundreds of feet before pulling the rip-cord. He didn't mention it in the official report, but all the other planes in the formation were zooming in around Lieutenant McAllister and him as they floated down, the pilots signaling their delight in their comrades' survival by coming, so Lindbergh thought, much too close to him for comfort. The only note of distress in the report has to do with the loss of his goggles and camera and the parachute's rip-cord; fliers who forgot to hold onto their rip-cords when they jumped were subjected to a prolonged razzing. "What? You threw away your rip-cord? And you want to be a flier?"

The third of Lindbergh's four emergency jumps is of significance to us because it resulted from the sort of mischance that he was afterwards to make sure would never befall him in the Spirit of St. Louis or in any of the planes with which he and Anne Lindbergh subsequently made exploratory flights throughout the world. Certain veteran "seat-of-the-pants" aviators tended to mock Lindbergh for the finicky caution he displayed in checking up on the smallest physical details of every plane he flew; he had learned to do so early and with reason. The official report of Lindbergh's third jump is as laconic as his report of the first; it is worth quoting in full because it describes

Lindbergh's plane in a wheat field.

Lambert Field, St. Louis, as it looked in the middle nineteen-twenties.

Once, flying the mail in a heavy fog at night, Lindbergh was unable to locate the Chicago airport. He flew until he ran out of gas, then jumped from the plane and parachuted down through the fog into a cornfield.

*Feb. 26, 1927*

## The Raymond Orteig $25,000 Prize
### PARIS · NEW YORK — NEW YORK · PARIS
*Trans-Atlantic Flight*

(Under the rules of the Fédération Aéronautique Internationale of Paris, France, and National Aeronautic Association of the United States of America of Washington, D. C.)

### ENTRY FORM

Name of Aviator Entrant (in full) __Charles A. Lindbergh,__

Address __% Mr. H. H. Knight, 401 Olive St., St. Louis, Missouri.__

Aviator's F. A. I. Certificate No.__6286__ Issued by __National Aeronautic Ass'n.,__

Aviator's Annual License No.__295 (1927)__ Issued by __National Aeronautic Ass'n.,__

PARTICULARS RELATING TO THE AIRCRAFT INTENDED TO BE USED.

Type, (Monoplane, Biplane, Hydroaeroplane, Flying Boat, etc.) *NYP Ryan Monoplane*

Wing area in sq. ft. *290* Load per sq. ft. *15½ lb.*

Make and type of engine *Wright J5 Whirlwind* Cu. in. Disp.

Approximate capacity of Fuel Tanks *425 gallons*

I, the undersigned, __Charles A. Lindbergh,__

of __% Mr. H. H. Knight, 401 Olive St., St. Louis, Mo.,__ hereby enter for the Raymond Orteig "New York-Paris" $25,000 Prize upon the following conditions :—

**1.** I agree to observe and abide by the Rules and Regulations for the time being in force and governing the contest, and to comply in all respects and at all times with the requests or instructions regarding the contest, which may be given to me by any of the Officials of the National Aeronautic Association of the United States of America.

**2.** In addition to, and not by the way of, limitation of the liabilities assumed by me by this entry under the said Rules and Regulations, I agree also to indemnify the National Aeronautic Association of the United States of America and the Trustees of the Raymond Orteig $25,000 Prize, and Mr. Raymond Orteig, the donor of the New York-Paris Flight Prize, or their representatives or servants, or any fellow competitor, against all claims and damages arising out of, or caused by, any ascent, flight or descent made by me whether or not such claims and demands shall arise directly out of my own actions or out of the acts, actions or proceedings of any persons assembling to witness or be present at such ascent or descent.

**3.** I enclose my certified check for $250.00 to the order of the Trustees of the Raymond Orteig $25,000 Prize, being Entrance Fee, and request to be entered on the Competitors' Register of the National Aeronautic Association of the United States of America.

Signature *Charles A. Lindbergh*

(Notary Seal.) Address *% Mr. Harry H. Knight*
*401 Olive St.*

Subscribed and sworn to before me
this 15th day of Feb. 1927. *St. Louis Mo.*

My commission expires

Date Feb. 15, 1927 *May 9-1927*

This blank is to be executed and forwarded with certified check to The Contest Committee of the National Aeronautic Association at No. 1623 H Street, Washington, D. C., and notice thereof immediately communicated to

The Secretary of the Trustees of the
Raymond Orteig Twenty-Five Thousand Dollar Prize
c/o Army and Navy Club of America

The entry form for the Orteig Prize.

the sort of flying common in the days when planes had few or no lights and traveled between airports that in most cases had no lights whatsoever. One's safety depended by day on an accurate knowledge of the terrain over which one was flying and, at night, of the constellations as well; a satisfactory means of flying entirely by instruments was still some years in the future. As the report reveals, Lindbergh was obliged to be in continuous eye contact with the ground, and this necessary intimacy was soon to stand him in good stead; less than a year later, out over the Atlantic on the way to Paris, he didn't hesitate to drop to within ten or fifteen feet of the stormy sea, in order to gauge the direction of the wind by the way in which foam was being blown off the crests of waves.

The third emergency jump took place on the night of October 4, 1926.

> I took off [so the report begins] from Lambert-St. Louis Field at 4:25 P.M. and after an uneventful trip arrived at Springfield, Ill., at 5:10 P.M. and Peoria, Ill., at 5:55 P.M.
>
> I took off from the Peoria Field at 6:10 P.M. There was a light ground haze but the sky was practically clear, containing only scattered cumulus clouds.
>
> Darkness set in about twenty-five miles northeast of Peoria and I took up a compass course, checking on the lights of the towns below until a low fog rolled in under me a few miles northeast of Marseilles and the Illinois River.
>
> The fog extended from the ground up to about six hundred feet and, as I was unable to fly under it, I turned back and attempted to drop a flare and land; but the flare did not function and I again headed for Maywood [the Chicago airport], hoping to find a break in the fog over the field.
>
> Upon examination I discovered that the cause of the flare failure was the short length of the release lever and that the flare might still be used by pulling the release cable.
>
> I continued on a compass course of fifty degrees until 7:15 P.M., when I saw a dull glow on the top of the fog, indicating a town below. There were several of these light patches on the fog, visible only when looking away from the moon, and I knew them to be the towns bordering the Maywood Field. At no time, however, was I able to locate the exact position of the field, although I understood that the searchlights were directed upwards and two barrels of gasoline burned in an endeavor to

attract my attention.

Several times I descended to the top of the fog, which was eight to nine hundred feet high according to my altimeter. The sky above was clear with the exception of scattered clouds and the moon and stars were shining brightly.

After circling around for thirty-five minutes, I headed west to be sure of clearing Lake Michigan and in an attempt to pick up one of the lights on the transcontinental [railroad] line.

After flying west for fifteen minutes and seeing no break in the fog, I turned southwest hoping to strike the edge of the fog south of the Illinois River.

Our ships carry 110 gallons of gasoline in the main tank and about nine in the reserve, which combined should supply a Liberty motor at cruising speed for fully five hours. That would make my time limit 9:30 P.M. and give me a twenty-minute warning of exhaustion when the main tank went dry and I switched on the reserve. Consequently, when the motor cut out at 8:20 P.M. and I cut in the reserve I expected to find low air-pressure or some other cause for cutting rather than a dry main tank. I was at the time only 1500 feet high and as the motor did not pick up as soon as I expected I shoved the flashlight in my belt and was about to release the parachute flare and jump when the engine finally took hold again.

A second trial showed the main tank to be dry and accordingly a maximum of twenty minutes' flying time left.

Several days later, I learned that the ship was the only one equipped with an eighty-five-gallon main tank. [The original one-hundred-and-ten-gallon tank had been removed because it was leaking and the mechanic who replaced it with an eighty-five-gallon tank had neglected to notify anyone of the difference in size.]

There were no openings in the fog and I decided to leave the ship as soon as the reserve tank was exhausted. I tried to get the mail pit open with the idea of throwing out the mail sacks and then jumping, but was unable to open the front buckle.

I knew that the risk of fire with no gasoline in the tanks was very slight and began to climb for altitude when I saw a light on the ground for several seconds. This was the first light I had seen for nearly two hours and as almost enough gasoline for fifteen minutes' flying remained in the reserve, I glided down to twelve hundred feet and pulled out the flare release cable as nearly as I could judge over the spot where the light had appeared. This time the flare functioned, but only to illuminate the top of a solid bank of fog, into which it soon disappeared without showing any trace of the ground.

Seven minutes' gasoline remained in the gravity tank. Seeing the glow of a town through the fog, I turned towards open country and nosed the plane up. At 5000 feet the motor sputtered and died. I stepped up on the cowling and out over the right side of the cockpit, pulling the rip-cord after about a hundred-foot fall. The parachute, an Irving seat-service type, functioned perfectly. I was falling head downward when the risers jerked me into an upright position and the chute opened. This time I saved the rip-cord.

I pulled the flashlight from my belt and was playing it down towards the top of the fog when I heard the plane's motor pick up. When I jumped, the motor had practically stopped dead and I had neglected to cut the switches. Apparently when the ship nosed down an additional supply of gasoline drained down into the carburetor. Soon the ship came into sight, about a quarter of a mile away and headed in the general direction of my parachute. I put the flashlight in a pocket of my flying suit preparatory to slipping the parachute out of the way if necessary. The plane was making a left spiral of about a mile in diameter and passed approximately three hundred yards away from my chute, leaving me on the outside of the circle.

I was undecided as to whether the plane or I was descending more rapidly and glided my chute away from the spiral path of the ship as quickly as I could.

The ship passed completely out of sight, but reappeared again in a few seconds, its rate of descent being about the same as that of the parachute. I counted five spirals, each one a little farther away than the last, before reaching the top of the fog bank.

When I settled into the fog, I knew that the ground was within 1000 feet and reached for the flashlight but found it missing. I could see neither earth nor stars and had no idea what kind of territory was below. I crossed my legs to keep from straddling a branch or wire, guarded my face with my hands, and waited.

Presently I saw the outline of the ground and a moment later was down in a cornfield. The corn was over my head and the chute was lying on top of the corn stalks. I hurriedly packed it and started down a corn row. The ground visibility was about one hundred yards.

In a few minutes I came to a stubble field and some wagon tracks, which I followed to a farmyard a quarter of a mile away. After reaching the farmyard, I noticed auto headlights and a spotlight playing over the roadside. Thinking that someone might have located the wreck of the plane, I walked over to the car. The occupants asked whether I had heard an airplane crash and it required some time to explain to them that I had been piloting the plane and yet was searching for it myself. I had to display the parachute as evidence before they were thoroughly convinced. The farmer was sure, as were most others within a three-mile radius, that the ship had just missed his house and crashed nearby. In fact, he could locate within a few rods the spot where he heard it hit the ground, and we spent an unsuccessful quarter of an hour hunting for the wreck in that vicinity before going to the farmhouse to arrange for a searching party and to telephone St. Louis and Chicago.

I had just put in the long-distance calls when the phone rang and we were notified that the plane had been found in a cornfield over two miles away.

It took several minutes to reach the site of the crash due to the necessity of slow driving through the fog, and a small crowd had already assembled when we arrived.

The plane was wound up in a ball-shaped mass. It had narrowly missed one farmhouse and had hooked its left wing in a grain shock a quarter of a mile beyond. The ship had landed on the left wing and wheel and had skidded along the ground for eighty yards, going through a fence before coming to rest on the edge of a corn field about a hundred yards short of a barn. The mail-pit was laid open and one sack of mail was on the ground. The mail, however, was uninjured.

The sheriff from Ottawa, Ill., arrived and we took the mail to the Ottawa Post Office to be entrained at 3:30 A.M. for Chicago.

In this report, as in the earlier one about the collision near Kelly Field, several characteristic notes are struck. One is the seeming equanimity with which Lindbergh sets about saving his life. He is lost in the fog a mile above the ground, he is soon to be running out of gas, and then, quite unexpectedly, he finds that he is already out of gas. Well, there you are! These things happen because other people are careless and forgetful, and when they happen they must be dealt with in as orderly a fashion as possible. He will be perfectly matter-of-fact in the face of disaster. He would like to toss the mail sacks out of the plane, but he cannot open the door into the mail pit. The motor cuts out and over the side of the plane he goes. Then he hears the motor starting up again and he realizes, to his chagrin, that he has been somewhat less matter-of-fact than he had intended to be. How could he have neglected to turn off the engine's switches? Now the plane had become a deadly missile, spiraling around him at close range. Even so, he remains calm and observant. Hanging in air under the great umbrella of his parachute, he coolly counts the number of spirals the abandoned plane executes around him before it vanishes into the fog.

Another characteristic note is the evident pleasure that Lindbergh has taken in writing the report. If he had wished, he could have told far less, but he has a storyteller's eye for the colorful, amusing detail; he cannot resist describing for us the strangers in the car and their incredulity when they learn that the young man asking them if they have seen a crashed plane is himself the pilot of the plane. He has to tell us, too, that the mail was uninjured ("uninjured," as if it were a person, and not merely undamaged) and was put aboard a train at 3:30 A.M. How exhausted he must have been by that time, having left St. Louis some eleven hours earlier and having so narrowly outwitted death! But he gives us no hint of personal discomfort: that would spoil the satisfaction he took in ending the report with the crucial word "Chicago." It was there that the mail had been intended to go and it was there that, however belatedly, it went.

Lindbergh was a writer. It is not how we tend to think of him at first, but there he stands, making his strong claim for our attention. Important as he would have been in history if he had not written a word, he is far more important because of the hundreds of thousands of words he wrote, most of which, without any loss of modesty, were about himself. We were sure, in any event, to have possessed the facts of his life, thanks to the unprecedentedly full documentation of him by the press. (On the morning after the flight to Paris, the New York <u>Times</u> devoted most of its first six pages to him and would later spread news of him over many eight-column banner headlines; that was the scale of the coverage that he received in newspapers here and abroad up to the outbreak of the Second World War.) But Lindbergh sought more for his place in history than a mere journalistic chronicle of his deeds; in a sense that he was loath to examine but not loath to embody, he wished his life to be seen to have a meaning and he wished for that meaning to prove instructive to others.

These were bold thoughts, and not the least remarkable thing about them was that Lindbergh came to them so early—certainly before the Paris flight, which from the beginning he saw as having two aspects, one private and the other public. He would attempt the crossing for his own sake, as being, in the eyes of a flier, the most superb adventure left on earth, but he would also attempt it for the sake of furthering the cause of aviation. And the suspicion that his talk of a cause might be only pious flummery and that his real purpose was fame and money was allayed by the fact that the actual Orteig Prize scarcely seemed to matter to him. Twenty-five thousand dollars ought to have struck a young man of small means as a considerable sum; Lindbergh ignored it, even to the point of violating the rules laid down by the National Aeronautics Association, which administered the Prize. Sixty days were supposed to pass between the time one was accepted as a contestant for the Prize and the time of one's departure for Paris. Lindbergh took off before his sixty days had passed, thus in principle (though not, as it turned out, in practice) forfeiting the Prize. The adventure and the cause: they were what prompted him and they sufficed. He was genuinely surprised when they were followed by fame and money.

To the end that his life might serve as an example, Lindbergh wrote copiously and collected copiously. At first, the writing required discipline, but the collecting always came easily. From earliest childhood, he had been an impassioned collector of objects—lead toy soldiers, coins, Indian arrowheads, semi-precious stones, and the like. The attic of the house in Little Falls was filled with his treasures, shelf upon shelf. As he grew older and his life took a more and more public bent, he began to squirrel away letters and pictures and newspapers and magazine clippings, and he commanded his mother, whenever she moved from one house to another, that she must take care to save everything. It was all of value, or might one day be found to be of value. As for him, he could throw nothing away. When the sheer mass of the letters, snapshots, and other memorabilia that Anne and he accumulated threatened to overwhelm their living space, he developed the habit of wrapping whatever they had no immediate use for in brown paper, tying it up with stout white string, and putting it away for safekeeping. Soon the brown paper packages were everywhere.

In the summer of 1941, the Lindberghs decided to turn over their family archives to the Sterling Memorial Library at Yale. They were living at the time at Lloyd Neck, Long Island. Lindbergh was at the height of his involvement with the America First Committee and was being regularly attacked by the Administration and by large sections of the press. In a passage taken from his <u>Wartime Journals</u> we can observe signs of the extreme emotional pressure he was under, though even in the privacy of his journals the control of his emotions never falters; we can also observe his improved skills as a writer:

> Spent the morning checking over diaries and other records and writing a letter to Knollenberg (Yale librarian). Anne and I have decided to turn our old files and records over to the Yale Library for safekeeping. These files and records contain material which should not be lost and some of which will be of interest in the future. We are making a provision that the boxes we send are not to be opened during our lifetimes without our authorization. We have considered various alternate dispositions that we might make of our files. In normal times I think we might keep them in the vaults and warehouses where they are at present. But in times such as we are now going through, when war may start next month and life itself is uncertain from one year to the next, I prefer to have our records in the safest possible location. I want them available in the future, both for ourselves and for our children.
>
> There are portions of everyone's life that could be improved if they could be lived again in the light of later experience; but Anne and I are not ashamed of the way we have lived our lives, and there is nothing in our records that we fear to

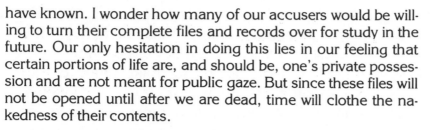

have known. I wonder how many of our accusers would be willing to turn their complete files and records over for study in the future. Our only hesitation in doing this lies in our feeling that certain portions of life are, and should be, one's private possession and are not meant for public gaze. But since these files will not be opened until after we are dead, time will clothe the nakedness of their contents.

After the war, the Lindberghs bought a big house on a wooded tract of land facing Long Island Sound, in Darien, Connecticut. It is a short journey by car from Darien to New Haven, and Lindbergh found it convenient from time to time to fill up some old wicker hampers and scuffed suitcases with papers and carry them off to the Sterling Memorial Library. He would always insist on carrying the hampers and suitcases down into the basement stacks unaided, so as not to inconvenience anyone. There are other sizeable deposits of Lindbergh material at the Missouri Historical Society, in St. Louis, and the Minnesota Historical Society, in St. Paul, as well as smaller deposits in Washington and elsewhere. It will be years if not decades before scholars can be sure of the total amount of Lindberghiana available to them.

The Lindbergh archives, still in the process of being catalogued, are estimated to number well over a million items, making them the most numerous of their kind at Yale. Included in the total are many thousands of letters that, over a period of almost fifty years, Lindbergh never got around to opening, much less answering. One such unopened letter is thought to have come from Einstein. Keepers of the Einstein papers have reason to believe that the letter was sent and they are curious to know what it contains, but the cataloguers have yet to turn it up. Lindbergh used to admonish friends to write their names in the upper left-hand corner of any envelopes addressed to him; he would hold a big batch of letters in his right hand, riffle them past his left thumb in a rapid gesture, and pick from the batch the names he recognized. Einstein and doubtless many other distinguished figures were unluckily not aware of Lindbergh's homely method of sorting his mail.

Until the archives at Yale and half a dozen other places

have been catalogued, no definitive biography of Lindbergh can be written. Lindbergh was aware that sooner or later such a biography would be called for, and on his deathbed he reluctantly gave his family permission to make whatever arrangements it might some day think feasible. His reluctance was that of a man who had never willingly relinquished to another any portion of his life; he dreaded the mistakes that would be sure to be made by a stranger attempting to master so vast an accumulation of documents; above all, he dreaded the speculation about motives and buried emotions that such a stranger would be tempted to make. To Lindbergh, securing an accurate likeness of a man by the exploration of his psyche was all moonshine. He did not wish to be accounted for in those terms. The dilemma was an old one for him—indeed, it had lasted a lifetime: on the one hand, to save everything, as if in readiness for the fullest possible public disclosure; on the other hand, to remain secret and disclose nothing. He would say with Emerson, "My life is not an apology, but a life. It is for itself and not for a spectacle." And he would hope that time would clothe as much of his nakedness as it revealed.

A stumbling block to all biographers of Lindbergh, whether past or future, is that the central event of his life—the event that pitched him headlong into history overnight—has been described with such verve and particularity by Lindbergh himself that no one can hope to better it. One reads lives of Lindbergh in which, at first uncannily, the heart of the book appears to be missing, and then one sees why this is so: the heart lies where it belongs, in the pages of <u>The Spirit of St. Louis</u>. When the book was published, in 1953, reviewers and the public at large were so struck by its high professional quality that they openly speculated upon the extent to which Anne Morrow Lindbergh, an author with an already established literary reputation, had helped her husband to write it. There were even rumors to the effect that she had been his ghost-writer—that the book was, in fact, hers and not his.

What a misreading of Lindbergh's nature those unflattering rumors amounted to! Proud man that he was, he would ask and accept her advice and would ask and accept the advice of many other persons as well (in the two pages of acknowledgements that are printed just before the preface of <u>Spirit</u>, Lindbergh thanks no fewer than thirty-six people for their criticism and suggestions in regard to the manuscript), but he would never have put his name to a book that was not from his hand. Indeed, so confident was he of his authorship that he was able to pay his wife a charming compliment in the dedication: "For A.M.L., who will never realize how much of this book she has written." Those are not the words of a man who fears to be seen to have depended overmuch upon a fellow-writer. They ring true as words of affection and gratitude.

The book is a literary tour de force. From beginning to end, it is written in what is known as the historical present indicative tense, which one is told as a student is an all but forbidden form in English. To be sure, an extremely skillful writer of fiction might risk it for a few pages in a short story, but for an extended work of autobiography, covering over five hundred closely printed pages—no, no, say the teachers, quite out of the question! In reference to the fact that Lindbergh always had to test everything for himself, even including the accuracy of weather reports, Anne Lindbergh once said of her husband, in a tone of mingled admiration and despair, "Nobody could ever tell Charles anything." Plainly nobody could tell him how he was to write his own life. He took a chance on the impermissible present indicative and brought it off in triumph; and his triumph was all the greater because the book had been written under unusually difficult circumstances.

Working in a pleasantly sequestered spot and drawing upon some Wordsworthian emotion "recollected in tranquillity," one might find it possible to sustain for a short period of time a certain mood and, matching it, a certain grammatical construction of a highly artificial nature, but Lindbergh, as he notes in his preface, was in an altogether different situation. He began the book in Paris, "during the tense prewar winter of 1938," and the manuscript was completed "on the shore of Scotts Cove, off Long Island Sound, in the hardly more tranquil year of 1952." In short, the book was fourteen years in the writing, and not only the times but the places in which it was written were of a remarkable dissimilarity.

> The chapters that follow [Lindbergh writes in his preface] have been drafted and revised under conditions ranging from the uncertainty of a fighting squadron's tent in the jungles of New Guinea, to the stable family life of a Connecticut suburban home, and under such diverse daily influences as accompany noonday, midnight, and dawn. On top of a manuscript sheet I often marked down my location at the moment of writing or revising. Glancing through old drafts, I now pick out, more or less at random, the following geographical positions: aboard S.S. Aquitana, en route Cherbourg to New York; Army and Navy Club, Washington, D.C.; with the Marines on a Marshall atoll; in a bomber, returning from the North Magnetic Pole; General Partridge's residence at Nagoya, Japan; in a house trailer on the Florida keys; on an air base in Arabia; parked on a roadside in the Italian Alps; camped in Germany's Taunus mountains; at the Carrels' Island of St. Gildas.

There was another and perhaps greater difficulty: the writing began more than eleven years after the last incident described in the book took place, and Lindbergh notes that this required him to draw heavily upon his memory for the early drafts. It would have been a considerable feat of intellect to produce a satisfactory account of his flight in the midst of so much traveling and with so little available documentation, but what Lindbergh produced was more than merely satisfactory—it was masterly. The long years that he spent on the project tempted him to make it increasingly ambitious. Evidently he had begun with the intention of telling how he had come to consider undertaking such a flight, how he had organized its financial details with his St. Louis backers, how he had commissioned the design of a new Ryan monoplane especially for his purposes, and then how, hour by hour for thirty-three and a half hours, he had flown above the Atlantic and over the French countryside to Le Bourget. At some point in the writing, it occurred to him to add brief interludes of family reminiscence—anecdotes about ancestors, episodes out of his childhood, and some of the chances and mischances of his growing up and finding a career.

These interludes begin about halfway through the book, in the section that is concerned with the actual flight. Lindbergh divides the section up into hours, and the first flashback of reminiscence emerges during the seventh hour, when the Spirit of St. Louis is speeding over Nova Scotia at a hundred miles an hour and Lindbergh is feeling optimistic. "Six hundred miles out. Three thousand miles to go. The columns of figures on my log sheet look impressive. When they grow six times that long, I should be over Paris." As usual, the prudent side of Lindbergh's nature immediately overcomes the ebullient side and begins a stern debate with it:

But I've got to be cautious about too much optimism. I'm at a point in my flight where I have the feeling of great accomplishment without having experienced the major strain of effort. In multiplying by six what I have done, I neglect the exponent of fatigue, and draw an arithmetical result from what is really a geometrical equation. Fatigue to a body is like air resistance to a plane. If you fly twice as fast (if you continue twice as long), you encounter four times the resistance (you become several times as tired).

That warning from Lindbergh to Lindbergh having been

The instrument panel. The photograph makes plain that Lindbergh had no forward visibility whatever and only imperfect visibility on either side.

The pilot's seat.

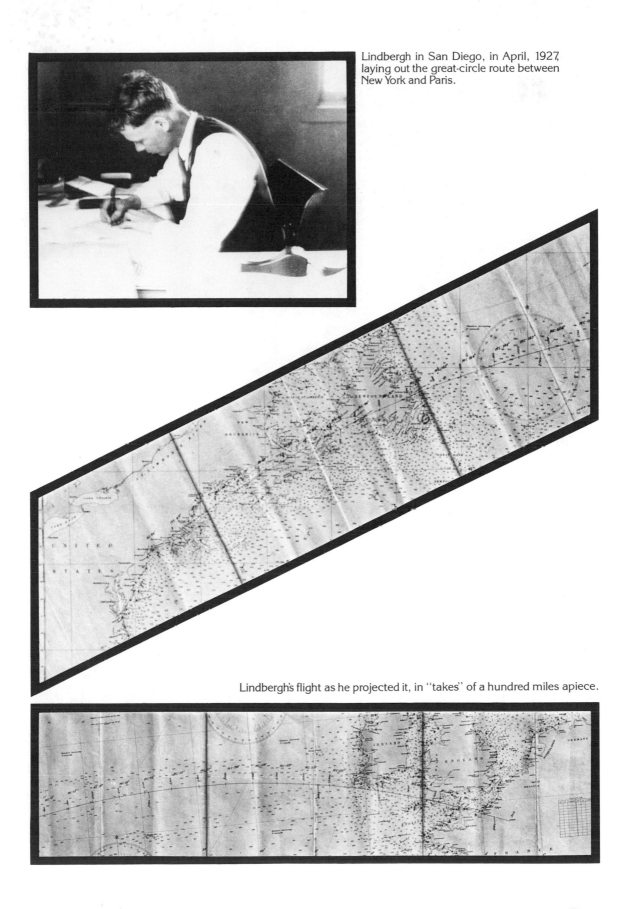

Lindbergh in San Diego, in April, 1927,
laying out the great-circle route between
New York and Paris.

Lindbergh's flight as he projected it, in ''takes'' of a hundred miles apiece.

An exchange of amenities for the sake of the press before the flight. Lindbergh, Byrd, and Chamberlin were the three leading contestants for the Orteig Prize on this side of the Atlantic. In France, Nungesser and Coli had already taken off from Le Bourget and had vanished without a trace. Byrd's left wrist is in a cast; he had broken it a few weeks before, in a test flight. Two weeks after Lindbergh's flight, Chamberlin and a passenger, Charles Levine, landed in Germany. In late June, Byrd and his crew of four came down in the sea off the coast of France.

Le Bourget, just outside Paris, a few days before Lindbergh landed there.

accepted, the author glances down and perceives a resemblance between the landscape over which he is flying and the landscape in which his father had grown up, in the Minnesota of the eighteen-sixties. "I think of childhood nights on the farm," he writes, "when I lay awake listening to my father's stories of hunting and trapping around such lakes as these. 'There were thousands of duck,' he had said, 'so many that the sky was blackened.' And there are thousands of duck below me, like a cloud's shadow drifting over land and water."

Throughout most of the remainder of the book, by a system of pretended free association less easygoing than it looks, Lindbergh weaves his way back and forth through time. The final reminiscence, in the twenty-sixth hour of the flight, brings him to the farm again. He remembers the last glimpse that he had of it, in the summer of 1923, when he landed his newly acquired Jenny in one of the pastures. Neither his mother nor father was there, and the house was padlocked. He was greeted by old Daniel Thompson, the Norwegian hired man. Axe on shoulder, Thompson inspected the plane and then said, "Nay doggone, the man that invented these things vas quite a feller!"

"How's the farm, Thompson?"

"All in veeds."

And Lindbergh reflects:

> I knew that day that childhood was gone. My farm on the Mississippi would become a memory, of which, sometime, I'd tell my children, just as my father told me of his fields and forests on Sauk River.

Here the author has assumed, not for the first or last time, the role of novelist, and so artfully that we scarcely notice it. He has put into the mind of an unmarried twenty-one-year-old (a young man who has yet to have his first date with a girl!) certain thoughts about his future parenthood, and we have to be on our guard to remember that the author himself at the time of writing is a middle-aged man who has married and become the father of six children, five of them living. The book must be read as, among many other things, a system of self-fulfilling prophecies; the flashbacks during the flight are literary inventions and express emotions colored by circumstances that arose long after the flight.

One advantage of writing as if by free association is that it permits an author to put into a book almost anything he pleases; another and probably greater advantage is that it permits him to leave out of a book almost anything he pleases. In the case of Spirit, Lindbergh makes interesting use of both options. He omits the darker passages in the family story—the parents' disintegrating marriage, the squabbles over property, the father's increasing financial difficulties, and his own failure at the university. A Tom Sawyer-like boyhood on the Mississippi is sketched in such a way as to seem more lyrical than it actually was. Indeed, the idyll that Lindbergh imposes on the lived reality causes a curious distortion in the treatment of his parents. He spent far more of his youth with his mother than with his father and always had far closer emotional ties with her, and yet it is the father who has become the chief figure in the author's recollections. The mother is made to play the conventionally second-class role of keeper of the house; she is a good cook and she takes her son for picnics in the woods and when he is sleepy she sings lullabies to him.

Evangeline Lindbergh lived long enough to read some of the manuscript of Spirit (she died in 1954, the year after it was published, but by then she was too ill to be aware of its contents), and one wonders whether, in looking over the early drafts, she may not have felt that the major share she took in Charles's upbringing had been skimped. Perhaps she understood, with the generosity of the survivor, that the long-dead father deserved to be remembered: the boy was not hers but theirs. They had trusted each other only in their unfaltering confidence in him.

Whatever the reason may be, a preference exists in Spirit that runs counter to our expectations. In the flashback where Lindbergh describes the burning of the house in Little Falls, it is the father that the frightened child cries out for first and afterward the mother. It is the father who, whistling in imitation of the call of a whippoorwill as he bicycles down the icehouse road to the farm, causes the waiting Charles to rush from the house and greet him. It is the father who calls the child "Boss" and asks what he can do to please him, whether it be to take him fishing or to carry him off on an expedition to the headwaters of the Mississippi. Under the best of circumstances, a mother would find it hard to compete with such adventures, but Evangeline contrived to do it at least twice—once, when she took Charles on a long sea-voyage to Panama, and again when, at Charles's urging, she allowed him to drive her brother and her to the West Coast and back. The Panama trip was a thrilling event to him at the time; he was ten and already a sedulous keeper of diaries. He wrote, "A alagator looks like a log when first seen" and "It seems that Mr. Taft has always had to admit he was rong it is very very queer." Nevertheless, he doesn't mention the voyage in Spirit, and he devotes only a few inconclusive words to the trip to California.

What Lindbergh chose to put into Spirit is likely to be more significant than what he left out—there are revelations, for example, that a self-confident author in his forties could afford to make that the fledgling author of We thought it wiser to suppress. Of these revelations, surely the most astonishing is Lindbergh's encounter with phantoms. In We there are no phantoms, possibly because Lindbergh was reluctant to let the public know that a hard-headed young aviator and champion of scientific progress believed in and could bear witness to the reality of the incorporeal. By the time he came to write Spirit, he had spent many years under the influence of Dr. Alexis Carrel, who as a leading member of the faculty of the Rockefeller Institute, in New York, found no difficulty in accepting an afterlife, communication with the dead, the authenticity of the miracles at Lourdes, and a dozen other scientifically unfashionable hypotheses concerning the nature of mind and matter.

When Lindbergh writes about the phantoms in Spirit, he does so with total conviction. In old age, in the pages of "Autobiography of Values," he returns to the phantoms and again treats their presence in his little plane out over the Atlantic as an unchallengeable certainty. They were simply and wonderfully there, all round him; they spoke with him, they gave him comfort, and then they vanished, and he was sorry to have them go. Their singular visitation took place in the twenty-second hour of the flight, at a time when Lindbergh was striving desperately to remain awake. He was flying through a dense fog and he often dropped to within a few feet of immense, storm-wracked, mid-ocean breakers, in an attempt to get beneath the fog. The attempt was always in vain. Meanwhile:

> Over and over again, I fall asleep with my eyes open, knowing I'm falling asleep, unable to prevent it; having all the sensations of falling asleep, as one does in bed at night; and then, seconds or minutes later, having all the sensations of waking up. When I fall asleep this way, my eyes are cut off from my ordinary mind as though they were shut, but they become directly connected to [a] new, extraordinary mind which grows increasingly competent to deal with their impressions. . . .

Oddly enough, in writing about the event so many years later, Lindbergh indicates no skepticism as to the origin of that new, extraordinary mind; he doesn't wish us to raise the question of whether it may have been merely a function of extreme fatigue. It is a mind genuinely new to him, genuinely extraordinary, and he believes in it as strongly in 1953 as he did in 1927. He flies with less anguish, he has his young self say, when his conscious mind is not awake. He feels that he has broken down the barrier between living and dreaming; in doing so, he has discovered an essential relationship between the two. "Some secret has been opened to me beyond the ordinary consciousness of man. Can I carry it with me beyond the flight, into normal life again? Or is it forbidden knowledge?"

And then exquisitely, not in haste, they arrive, his new acquaintances. The fuselage behind him is filled with ghostly presences. They are vague in outline and transparent—he can observe them without turning his head, for his skull has become a single large eye, capable of seeing everywhere at once. The phantoms begin to speak and their voices have a welcomely human pitch and timbre. "First one and then another presses forward to my shoulder to speak above the engine's noise, and then draws back among the group behind. At times, voices come out of the air itself, clear yet far away, traveling through distances that can't be measured by the scale of human miles; familiar voices, conversing and advising on my flight, discussing problems of my navigation, reassuring me, giving me messages of importance unattainable in ordinary life."

Lindbergh continues to speak of the phantoms in this perfervid vein for many hundreds of words; they are a matter of great importance to him at that moment and will continue to be so always, but for the reader who has never encountered phantoms and has thought of Lindbergh as the epitome of the rational they introduce a number of unresolved mysteries. The tone of the passage is not that of science but of science fiction. Again and again we wish to interrupt the author with the kind of matter-of-fact questions that Lindbergh himself might be expected to ask when confronted with such a cat's cradle of hinted-at profundities. What scale of "miles" can one speak of except a human scale? What is "familiar" about the phantoms' voices, given that he has never listened to phantoms before? Plainly they ought to be good at flying, but what advice on flying do they actually give him? When it comes to navigation, phantoms are surely more skillful than mortals; what help did they give Lindbergh with his problems? Most fascinating of all, what messages of importance "unattainable in ordinary life" did they bring to him? One usually thinks of messages as either receivable or unreceivable; why does Lindbergh use the word "unattainable"?

These are legitimate questions and there are no answers to them, either in <u>Spirit</u> or in the "Autobiography of Values." Writing in the "Autobiography" a year before his death, Lindbergh describes again the fog above the Atlantic and his fatigue on "the only occasion in my life when I saw and conversed with ghosts. . . . I can still see those phantoms clearly in memory, but after I landed at Paris I could not remember a single word they said." He is well aware of the recklessness of this confession. He knows that his ghosts will be said to be hallucinations, the ravings of an exhausted brain. "My visions are easily explained away through reason," he wrote, "but the

longer I live, the more limited I believe rationality to be. . . . Certainly my visions in the Spirit of St. Louis entered into the reality of my life, for they stimulated thought along new lines: thought enters into both the creation and the definition of reality. . . .I recognized that vision and reality interchange, like energy and matter."

One races through the pages of Spirit as if it were a series of stop-press newspaper bulletins—as if, hour after hour, the outcome of that unprecedented flight were still in doubt. And what makes Lindbergh's accomplishment even more impressive than it is commonly reckoned to be is that the flight was, except for a single mischance, so easy. Easy? It is an unlikely word for an attempt that, up to then, had always ended in death, and yet it is one of the underlying themes of the book that Lindbergh and Donald Hall, the designer of the plane, had anticipated every contingency so well that in mechanical terms nothing of importance did go wrong throughout the flight. In their view, once the plane was off the ground at Roosevelt Field and headed in the direction of Paris, there was no reason whatever that it wouldn't eventually get there. For on the way to the drawing board the problem had been a simple one to state: design a plane that at take-off could lift gasoline enough to fly four thousand miles. After that, everything depended on the pilot.

In a few seconds on the morning of May 20, 1927, it turned out that Lindbergh and Hall had provided such a plane. The weather on the flight was foul, but it was no worse than the weather Lindbergh had often encountered flying the mail between St. Louis and Chicago. The Great Circle route that Lindbergh had laid out in hundred-mile "takes" looked, on his crudely inked chart, like the handiwork of a child; nevertheless, it proved so accurate that, coupled with his superb navigation, the Spirit of St. Louis made landfall almost exaclty on target, at Dingle Bay on the southwest coast of Ireland. Lindbergh had estimated that he might reach Europe as much as four hundred miles off course; that was why he had asked for a range of four thousand miles. Landing in Paris, he could not resist boasting that the gas remaining in his tanks would have carried him as far as Rome.

The single damnable mischance that put the flight in jeopardy was Lindbergh's having gone without sleep the night before he took off. He had calculated on forty hours in the air and he was aware from previous experience that he could readily manage to remain alert for that length of time. What he had not calculated on was having to remain alert for sixty-three hours. It was wholly unlike him to have allowed this dangerous situation to arise; for once, he had given way to pleasurable self-indulgence, and he never forgot that the price of it might well have proved to be his life. He had been ready to take off on Monday, May 16, but the weather was unpromising. On Thursday, the weather reports continued to be so discouraging that Lindbergh and some friends left the Spirit of St. Louis under guard at the field on Long Island and went off to visit the Wright factory in Paterson, New Jersey, and to spend some time at the house of Guy Vaughan, a vice-president of the Wright company. That evening, Lindbergh and his party had been invited to attend a performance of the hit musical Rio Rita, in New York. They were to see the show from backstage—a novelty for Lindbergh and a mark of his growing celebrity.

As they were driving to the theatre, the Lindbergh party stopped on an impulse and telephoned the Weather Bureau. They learned that the weather over the Atlantic was unexpectedly clearing; there was a chance that Lindbergh would be able to take off at daybreak. They abandoned their plans for the theatre and went out to the field to get the plane ready. By the time Lindbergh returned to his hotel in Garden City and prepared to go to bed, it was close to midnight. He would have two and a half hours in which to sleep. He posted a friend outside his bedroom door with instructions to keep everyone away (earlier, a number of reporters and autograph-seekers had waylaid him in the hotel lobby) and to wake him at 2:15 A.M. He got into bed and to his surprise remained wakeful; usually he fell asleep the moment his head struck the pillow. Minutes passed, and he was just about to doze off; suddenly, there was a knock on the door. It was his friend, who came in and sat down on the edge of Lindbergh's bed. The friend, who was from out of town, was looking puzzled. "Slim," he said, "what am I going to do when you're gone?"

Propping himself up on one elbow, Lindbergh cannot believe his ears—his friend has come in at this unlikely hour to ask such a question as that? Patiently, Lindbergh says, "I don't know. There are plenty of other problems to solve before we have to think about that one." He sends his friend away, but now he is wide awake. He knows that he will be unable to sleep. His mind races. He lies there, waiting.

The Spirit of St. Louis was serialized in The Saturday Evening Post under the title "Thirty-three and a Half Hours." It was a Book-of-the-Month Club selection and immediately upon publication it became a best seller. It won a Pulitzer Prize and was sold to Warner Brothers, who made it into a movie starring Jimmy Stewart. All told, the book was reported to have netted Lindbergh well over a million dollars. Privately, Lindbergh said that the sum was much less than that, but no matter—it had been a long time since he had concerned himself with getting any richer than he was. The important thing to him was the nature and quality of the achievement. He had always liked bringing something off against the highest possible odds. On his very first parachute jump, he had decided to try a double jump instead of a single one (the second parachute had almost failed to open). In a rickety old Army biplane that was having difficulty enough getting from St. Louis to Chicago, he had first thought, "Why shouldn't I fly from New York to Paris?" That boy struggling in agony to stay awake above the Atlantic had landed in high spirits at Le Bourget. Now the boy, grown to middle age, had turned his memories of the flight into a successful work of art. It would be hard to say which was the more remarkable feat.

The main text of <u>The Spirit of St. Louis</u> ends abruptly, with an exclamation—"But the entire field ahead is covered with running figures!" In a brief "Afterword," Lindbergh hints at a possible sequel to the book: "The welcome I received at Le Bourget was only a forerunner to the welcome extended by France, by Belgium, by England—and, through messages, by all of Europe. It was a welcome which words of appreciation are incompetent to cover. But the account of my experiences abroad, of my homecoming to the United States, and of my gratitude to the peoples of Europe and America, belongs to a different story."

No such story came to be written, but in the "Autobiography of Values" there are many glimpses of the events out of which it could have been composed. To Parisians in those first few days after the flight, the most extraordinary thing about Lindbergh was the grace and good humor with which he accepted the tumultuous acclamation of uncounted tens of thousands—soon to be millions—of total strangers. How could this shy loner, this inward-looking, "unheralded" boy have learned to respond with such tact to a wholly unexpected outpouring of affection on the part of a people whose customs and very language were unknown to him? Was it a matter of his receiving excellent coaching from Ambassador Herrick and his staff at the Embassy, where Lindbergh was a guest? Not likely, for at every turn there were opportunities for the young man to make a blunder by means of a single unlucky word or gesture, and he never did so.

The truth was complex and implausible. Lindbergh had arrived at Le Bourget assuming that, because he was ahead of schedule, there would be no one there to meet him. He would identify himself to the authorities, arrange (by sign language if necessary) for his plane to be placed in a hangar, and then ask a flying colleague at the field for assistance in making his way to Paris and securing accommodations at some inexpensive hotel. He had concentrated hard on the flight itself and had ignored its consequences. But even if he had considered what a visit to Paris would require in the way of clothing, he would have been unable to make any provision for it. He had weighed not by the pound but by the ounce and half-ounce every article of gear that he judged it necessary to carry aboard the plane. Grudgingly, he had consented to the weight of an inflatable rubber raft, but not to the weight of a parachute: the raft would be useful if he were forced down at sea, while a parachute would be useful only over land, and there would be mighty little of that between New York and Paris. He had also put aboard four red flares, a canteen of water, five cans of Army emergency rations, a hunting knife, a ball of cord, a ball of string, two fish hooks, a large needle, a flashlight, a match-safe with matches, a hack-saw blade, and an Armburst cup, by means of which salt water could be turned into fresh. A suit, some shirts, ties, socks, and underwear, a razor, even a toothbrush— to have added that much weight to the plane was out of the question, because it would have reduced his maximum range by many miles. Lindbergh arrived in Paris with the clothing he had on his back, empty-handed except for a few uneaten sandwiches in a brown paper bag.

The crowds at Le Bourget stunned Lindbergh. Unbeknownst to him, word of his approach along the valley of the Seine had been reaching Paris by telegraph and telephone from the moment he had been sighted over the harbor at Cherbourg. It appeared that all Paris had set out for the field to welcome him, leading to the greatest traffic jam in Paris history. He touched down at 10:22 P.M., Paris time, and while he was still taxiing across the field thousands of cheering people began to press in around the plane. He gives an account in <u>We</u> of the hurly-burly of his arrival; it is more good-natured than he was feeling at the time. Of course he was joyful that he had achieved his goal, but his little plane was threatened with being destroyed by souvenir-hunters and he himself, for a time, was in serious danger. For him and his plane to have survived the longest and most difficult flight in history and then to be mauled and broken up by unthinking well-wishers—! He suppressed the bitterness of that irony in <u>We</u>, though he was still husbanding it in his heart nearly fifty years later.

I cut the switch [he writes in <u>We</u>] to keep the propeller from killing someone, and attempted to organize an impromptu guard for the plane. The impossibility of any immediate organization became apparent, and when parts of the ship began to crack from the pressure of the multitude I decided to climb out of the cockpit in order to draw the crowd away.

Speaking was impossible; no words could be heard in the uproar and nobody apparently cared to hear any. I started to climb out of the cockpit, but as soon as one foot appeared through the door I was dragged the rest of the way without any assistance on my part.

For nearly half an hour I was unable to touch the ground, during which time I was ardently carried around in what seemed to be a very small area, and in every position it is possible to be in. Everyone had the best of intentions but no one seemed to know just what they were.

The French military flyers very resourcefully took the situation in hand. A number of them mingled with the crowd; then, at a given signal, they placed my helmet on an American correspondent and cried: "Here is Lindbergh." That helmet on an American was sufficient evidence. The correspondent immediately became the center of attraction, and while he was being taken protestingly to the Reception Committee via a rather devious route, I managed to get inside one of the hangars.

Meanwhile a second group of soldiers and police had surrounded the plane and soon placed it out of danger in another hangar.

Ambassador Herrick and other members of a hastily assembled Reception Committee had been waiting for Lindbergh in another part of the field. The false Lindbergh having been ushered in to him and dismissed, Herrick was at last brought face to face with the authentic Lindbergh. A charming, affectionate man in his seventies, Herrick fell at once under the young man's spell. He invited Lindbergh to "come home" with him to the Embassy and Lindbergh accepted the invitation. It can be argued that it was the acceptance of that unexpected invitation which marked the true turning point in Lindbergh's life. From the moment that he fell asleep in a big bedroom at the Embassy, wearing a pair of pajamas borrowed from the Ambassador, Lindbergh was never to occupy the world of his youth again. A signal of his crossing from one world to another was the tender and whimsical telegram that Ambassador Her-

*Spirit of St. Louis* immediately after arrival at Le Bourget.

rick dispatched to Evangeline Lindbergh in Detroit: "Warmest congratulations. Your incomparable son has honored me by becoming my guest. He is in fine condition and sleeping sweetly under Uncle Sam's roof. Myron T. Herrick."

When Lindbergh woke, early in the afternoon of Sunday, the 22nd of May, he found Blanchard, the Ambassador's valet, standing by his bedside. A bath, Blanchard announced, had been drawn. Blanchard having raised the window-shades, Lindbergh observed what he had been too sleepy to take note of on tumbling into bed some nine or ten hours earlier—the immaculate white sheets and silky quilt that had been covering him. The room, he thought at once, was like those he had seen in movies, back in the States: a room in a palace, different from any he had ever encountered in real life.

Blanchard held out a bathrobe and to Lindbergh the gesture was again movie-like, fantastic. He had never owned a bathrobe; he had considered it a totally superfluous article of clothing. He got out of bed and slipped his arms into the sleeves of the robe and Blanchard pointed the way to the bathroom. On a chair in the bathroom, beside a tub half-filled with warm water, lay a pair of socks, turned halfway inside out in order to make them easier to put on. Another fantastic gesture! Breakfast would be brought to him, Blanchard said, as soon as he had finished his bath. How did he like his eggs?

Lindbergh wrote long afterwards that it had been a formidable challenge, adjusting to a valeted and butlered life, but he had resolved at once to do his best to meet it—indeed, Ambassador Herrick was so fatherly and hospitable and the rest of the Herrick family took him in so readily and made so much of him that there was no alternative. At a single bound, between sleeping and waking, he had passed not only from comparative obscurity to international fame but also from the small, servantless houses he had known in Little Falls and Detroit and St. Louis to the great houses of the very rich, and he would rarely be far from them in the future. He would not frequent them but he would enter them with assurance and would be grateful for the privacy they provided. Though he would never live as the rich did, under the tyranny of innumerable possessions and endless rounds of idle partygoing, he would share with them the high value they placed upon the freedom to be themselves.

That first day at the Embassy had many moments of comedy. Lindbergh's clothes consisted of twill breeches, a heavy shirt, tan leather boots, and high wool socks—no doubt an ideal costume for flying but unsuitable, it was suggested to him, for the mounting number of official and unofficial ceremonies that were being planned in his honor. The problem was solved by the resourceful Blanchard (who was to advance over the years from gentleman's gentleman to the post of steward in the grandest of New York houses, where after long service he died on duty, quietly, giving no trouble to anyone). It turned out that Blanchard had a friend from whom he was able to borrow a business suit that came close to fitting Lindbergh—"a little baggy around the shoulders and a bit short in the pants. . . . I would not have to wear that suit very long, though, because a tailor had been found who would take my measurements and make the clothes I needed immediately. He was an Englishman, with a shop in Paris. He would put aside his other work, and he could finish my first suit by the next afternoon. But of course I would need several suits and a tail-coat."

Lindbergh reasoned that once he had consented to conform, he might as well conform entirely; the black evening ties and white evening ties and stiff-collared "boiled" shirts and shiny patent-leather shoes that accompanied his suits seemed quite in keeping with the bizarre public life that he had now embarked upon. Examining in the mirror the transformation that Blanchard and others had worked on his person, he shook his head: "With a high collar poking up my chin and pearl studs glowing on my chest, I realized with some pangs of conscience the disdain with which my previous self would have viewed my [new] existence."

There would be no turning back from the role he had so quickly embraced, and no temporary turning aside from it. "I was astonished at the effect my successful landing in France had on the nations of the world. To me, it was like a match

Outside the United States Embassy in Paris, the day after the flight. Ambassador Myron T. Herrick is leading the cheers.

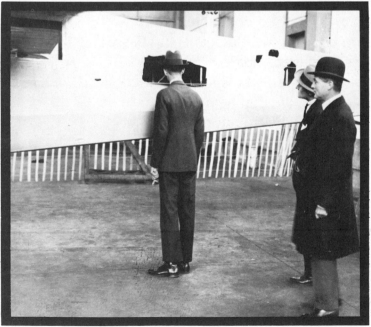

Later in the day, Lindbergh inspects the damage done to his plane by souvenir-seekers. He is wearing a borrowed suit.

Back home in America, Lindbergh's mother is given a reception by thirty-five hundred students at the Cass Technical High School, in Detroit, where she teaches chemistry. She is accompanied by her uncle, John C. Lodge, then Acting Mayor of Detroit.

A representative sampling of the keys to the city bestowed upon Lindbergh in the course of the months following his flight. The key to the city of Paris (Number One) is remarkably small; the keys to the cities of Buffalo (Number Four), Chelsea (Number Seven), and Boise, Idaho (Number Eleven) are remarkably large.

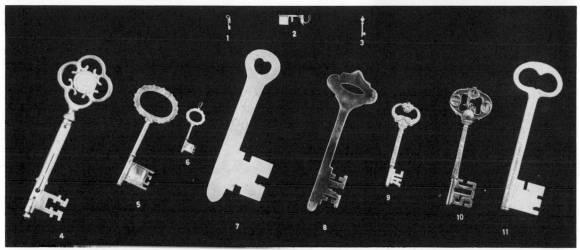

A reception in Paris.

lighting a bonfire. I thought thereafter that people confused the light of the bonfire with the flame of the match, and that one individual was credited with doing what, in reality, many groups of individuals had done." He wrote those words in his sixties, not in the least out of false modesty; they seemed to him, after a lifetime of reflection, to embody a truth that, modest as it was, he had struggled hard to give an accurate, lasting definition to. And it was this: that the cultural evolution of the life of a group can be profoundly affected by changes in the cultural evolution of the life of an individual, especially to the extent that such an individual departs from the conventional aspirations of the group. A man's life gains value and becomes exemplary when in the course of fulfilling himself he happens to offer the group of which he has been a part the opportunity to fulfill itself.

In Lindbergh's case, a single bold deed, undertaken primarily as a personal adventure, was proving of intense emotional interest to the whole world. What would be the consequences of this emotion? Would they be good or evil? At twenty-five, Lindbergh would have answered unhesitatingly that they would be good; at sixty-five, he would have shrugged and said he couldn't be sure.

The cost to him of his new life would be high: Lindbergh saw instantly that a new environment, charged with new opportunities, meant also a host of new responsibilities. This would be the case even in respect to his always uneasy relations with the press. There would never be peace between him and them; there would be only an armed truce. It had been difficult enough for him to pose for newspaper and newsreel photographers when he had something constructive to do—put mail sacks into a plane heading for Peoria and Chicago, put gasoline into the Spirit of St. Louis at Curtiss Field. Now, on the afternoon of his very first day in Paris, Parmely Herrick, the Ambassador's son, asked him if he would mind stepping out on the balcony of the Embassy, in order that the hundreds of men and women who had been waiting for hours in the street outside the Embassy to catch a glimpse of him might at last be granted their wish.

The prospect of being put on personal exhibition embarrassed and disturbed Lindbergh. It was something novel to him, totally unlike the exhibitions of wing-walking and parachute-jumping that he had been accustomed to give in his barnstorming days. On those occasions, it was a man's skill and daring that the crowd applauded; the man himself was secondary. Afterwards, it was amusing for a time to be slapped on the back and looked up to as a daredevil, but one was always aware of being part of a team, which consisted of the plane, the pilot who flew the plane, and the parachute that saved one's life. To stand like a grinning mannequin on a balcony, while people stared and shouted and clapped their hands—that was unnatural and unnerving and Lindbergh consented to it on that Sunday afternoon only because the gesture pleased the Ambassador and Parmely Herrick. Indeed, the Ambassador appeared to enjoy the situation immensely; he kept on waving and cheering along with the crowd.

How much more tolerable it would be, Lindbergh thought, if there were something constructive for him to say! But he spoke not a word of French and he supposed that very few in the crowd spoke a word of English. Someone in the Ambassadorial party suggested that he announce that he was glad to be in France. What could be triter and more unsatisfactory than that, even if he could utter the statement in perfect French? "I just stood there," he wrote subsequently, in an unpublished note, "while my face got red and I said nothing. I realized it was a great honor, and I was deeply touched by the ovation; but I slipped in off the balcony as soon as I could with tact."

Lindbergh's first and most profound transformation took place when he chose flying as a profession. His second transformation took place during those early days in Paris. In the midst of incessant festivities, he was able with remarkable prescience to observe the outlines of a future life very different from any he had anticipated. And it was a life about which he felt at once certain grave doubts: the mannequin on the balcony was not only grinning but thinking. The thirty-three and a half hours he had spent in the air between New York and Paris had not changed him by an iota—they had only intensified in him the very characteristics that had prompted him to undertake the flight—but the first thirty-three and a half hours of his stay in Paris threatened to bestow on him a new and not necessarily welcome career. He would have to act fast in order to prevent simple good manners from amounting, in the world's eyes, to an unprotesting acceptance of that career.

By an irony, the success of a single act of daring had begun to impose on Lindbergh's unaltered nature responsibilities as heavy in their fashion as the responsibilities that had been imposed on it by a whole series of failures—the failure of his parents' relationship, of his attempt at farming, of his wasted years of schooling. He would try to shoulder the burdens of success as manfully as he had shouldered those of failure, but that was not to say that he would consent to the unappealing role that he saw being thrust upon him in his sudden fame. Was it expected of him that he serve as a sort of icon, a passive object of worship to the multitude? Gracefully, he rejected the role and improvised another in its place. That rigorous shaping of himself that he had practiced since boyhood required continuous bodily action and an unquestioned freedom of movement (he always preferred telling where he had been to where he was going). If henceforth much of his life was to have the disadvantage of being lived in public, at least he would try to make sure that it was a life of spontaneous deeds and not a permanent throned entrapment.

To that end, Lindbergh set about externalizing his superb adventure; at every opportunity, he drew attention to the bonfire and not to the match. Whenever speeches were given in his honor, whether at first in Paris and Brussels and London, or later in Washington and New York and St. Louis, and he was called upon to make a reply, he would speak not about himself but about international good will and the future of aviation. Listening to his brief, impersonal messages, people praised him for his modesty, and he deserved their praise, but he was also setting strict limits upon the uses to which he was willing to be put: this far would he go and no further. He was civil, he was charmingly at ease, with kings, queens, and assorted ministers of state and other dignitaries. (George V of England is said to have asked, at a private audience, how Lindbergh relieved himself during the flight and Lindbergh is said to have answered readily that he had made use of a funnel and an aluminum container, placed directly under a gap in his wicker chair; the container was disposed of somewhere over France. His Majesty, an old Navy man, appears to have been grateful to receive a sensible answer to a sensible question.) Lindbergh was greeted everywhere by demonstrations of emotion appropriate to the coming of some long-awaited god; he responded to these feverish demonstrations with an ungodlike friendliness of demeanor and a few cool words. The fewness of the words, as well as their coolness, led to still greater outbursts of hysteria.

At a luncheon attended by several hundred Americans in Paris, Lindbergh was effusively lauded by a succession of speakers. His reply took less than a minute:

> Gentlemen, 132 years ago Benjamin Franklin was asked: "What good is your balloon? What will it accomplish?" He replied: "What good is a new born child?" Less than twenty years ago when I was not far advanced from infancy M. Blériot flew across the English Channel and was asked "What good is your aeroplane? What will it accomplish?" Today those same skeptics might ask me what good has been my flight from New York to Paris. My answer is that I believe it is the forerunner of a great air service from America to France, America to Europe, to bring our peoples nearer together in understanding and in friendship than they have ever been.

Ambassador Herrick had provided Lindbergh with the anecdote about Franklin, and M. Blériot, who was seated with him on the dais, had no doubt furnished the questions concerning his pioneer flight across the Channel. In print, Lindbergh's remarks seem unlikely to bring a large audience to its feet cheering and shouting his name, but they did so with ease. And for years to come, any words he chose to utter would produce the same disproportionately tumultuous results.

Whether Lindbergh spoke or kept silent, his presence sufficed in those first Paris days to make people happy. Back home in America, his countrymen grew increasingly impatient for his return. Day after day, banner headlines carried news of his triumphs abroad, and this was all very well—it was high time that the inhabitants of the Old World showed some respect for the miracle-working inhabitants of the New—but Lindbergh belonged among his own people. He must allow them to make a demonstration of affection and pride, which, in true American style, would be sure to surpass the most fervent of European demonstrations.

Rumors began to appear in the press to the effect that Lindbergh intended to drift around Europe for a time and then fly back to the States by way of Asia. That would be a journey of many weeks' duration, with no telling what unknown hazards to be faced along the way; moreover, it would give everyone else in the world a chance to see and praise him before his fellow-citizens could do so. This was manifestly unfair. Soon there were letters in the newspapers asking high officials in the government to intercede with Lindbergh. The future plans of the once unheralded boy appeared on the agenda of the Executive Offices of the White House and were the subject of lively debate. Lindbergh had been a Captain in the Officers Reserve Corps, and one of the first fruits of his flight was his promotion to a full Colonelcy. Colonel Lindbergh was subject to the authority of the Commander in Chief, who was the President of the United States. The Secretary of War, the Secretary of the Navy, and the Secretary of State all urged that the President act at once.

With unaccustomed alacrity, President Coolidge took charge of the problem. He ordered that a U.S. Navy cruiser be dispatched post-haste to France to pick up the young man and his plane and bring them home to glory.

Just before noon on Saturday, June 11, 1927, the U.S.S. Memphis came alongside the Navy Yard dock in Washington, D.C. Cannon boomed salutes, planes roared overhead, and a vast crowd, held back by Marines with fixed bayonets, cheered as Admiral Burrage, commander of the Memphis, walked down the gangplank and, a few moments later, ascended the gangplank with Evangeline Lindbergh on his arm. The crowd was enchanted: his mother! The hero's mother! Her unexpected appearance had the magical appropriateness of an episode in a fairy tale. After a few minutes, mother and son came down the gangplank and were greeted by a formidable assortment of dignitaries, including the Secretary of War, the Secretary of the Navy, the Postmaster General, and a former Secretary of State, the bearded and august Charles Evans Hughes. The crowd broke through the Marine cordon and attempted to surround the Lindberghs. They were hurried away into a waiting open car and taken by a parade escort of cars, motorcycles, and cavalry through the streets of Washington. It was a hot, sunny day, and the crowd that had gathered to welcome Lindbergh was incomparably the largest in Washington's history.

In a stand that had been built for the occasion near the Washington Monument, President and Mrs. Coolidge, flanked by scores of diplomats and government officials, shook hands with the Lindberghs. Coolidge then stepped to the lectern to begin his official address of welcome, carried by radio to the country at large. Coolidge and Lindbergh had in common a preference for terseness of speech and for showing as little emotion in public as possible. But Coolidge, unlike Lindbergh, had no gift for words. He was a master of the self-evident observation. (Years later, he was to write, "When large numbers of men are out of work, unemployment results.") In his thin-sounding Yankee voice, he uttered commonplaces with the authority of an epigrammatist. His welcome to Lindbergh was a Coolidge classic in every respect save its great length, which was so unusual that reporters attributed it to the extreme emotion felt by the President. The speech began:

My Fellow-Countrymen:

It was in America that the modern art of flying heavier-than-air machines was first developed. As the experiments became successful, the airplane was devoted to practical purposes. It has been adapted to commerce in the transportation of passengers and mail and used for national defense by our land and sea forces.

Beginning with a limited flying radius, its length has been gradually extended. We have made many flying records. Our Army fliers have circumnavigated the globe.

Given that the sky over Washington had been filled with planes since early morning, this primer-like account of the origin of aviation must have struck Lindbergh and many other members of the President's audience as singularly unnecessary. The President plodded on. Having praised the Army for circumnavigating the globe, he felt obliged to say something in praise of the Navy as well, but the compliment proved an unfortunate one: "One of our Navy men started from California and flew far enough to have reached Hawaii, but being off course, landed in the water."

Only literal-minded Coolidge would have thought to speak of that hapless Navy flier in the presence of Lindbergh, who, three weeks earlier, had remained precisely on course through long hours of blind flying in rain, sleet, fog, high winds, and darkness. Many hundreds of gratuitous words later ("And now, my fellow-citizens, this young man has returned. He is here..."), Coolidge brought his address to a close by pinning on Lindbergh's chest the Distinguished Flying Cross. Lindbergh ducked his head towards the microphones on the lectern and spoke even more briefly than he had in Paris; his remarks lasted approximately half a minute:

On the evening of May 21, I arrived at Le Bourget, France. I was in Paris for one week, in Belgium for a day and was in London and in England for several days. Everywhere I went, at every meeting I attended, I was requested to bring a message home to you. Always the message was the same.

"You have seen," the message was, "the affection of the people of France for the people of America demonstrated to you. When you return to America, take back that message to the people of the United States from the people of France and of Europe.

I thank you.

Members of the audience remained silent for a time, waiting for more; when they perceived that Lindbergh's speech was indeed over, they burst into prolonged applause. Afterwards, the press was quick to draw a comparison between the stunned silence that followed Lindbergh's speech and the stunned silence that is said to have followed Lincoln's speech at Gettysburg, but from the vantage point of half a century later it appears that the two silences were of different kinds. That evening Lindbergh was honored by the National Press Club, at a meeting held in the Washington Auditorium. The night air was sweltering, but six thousand people eagerly squeezed their way into the building. A dozen or so speeches and messages were delivered by members of the Cabinet and representatives of foreign governments, and at last Lindbergh got up to make a general reply. This time his remarks were, for him, extended—they went on for three or four minutes and were devoted to a summary of the separate courses being followed by American and European aviation. "All Europe looks on our air mail service with reverence," he said. "There is nothing like it anywhere abroad.

"But, whereas we have mail lines, they have passenger lines. All Europe is covered with a network of lines carrying passengers between all the big cities. Now it is up to us to create and develop passenger lines that compare with our mail routes...."

To a student of Lindbergh, the most important part of his talk consists of its two opening paragraphs. They are in a mildly humorous vein, and the audience enjoyed them so much that he was to make use of them several times thereafter—the wise husbandry of a man who must endure hearing his praises sung on a hundred similar occasions and must then find some civil way of acknowledging them.

I want to express my appreciation [he began] of the reception I've met in America and the welcome I have received here

Crowds in Washington breaking through Marine and police barriers as Lindbergh arrives aboard the U.S.S. *Memphis.*

Lindbergh approaching New York in the official city yacht, *Macom.*

tonight. When I landed at Le Bourget a few weeks ago, I landed with the expectancy and hope of being able to see Europe. It was the first time I had ever been abroad. I had seen a number of interesting things when I flew over Ireland and Southern England and France. I had only been gone from America two days or a little less, and I wasn't in any particular hurry to get back.

But by the time I had been in France a week, Belgium a day and England two or three days—by that time I had opened several cables from America and talked with three Ambassadors and their attachés and found that it didn't make much difference whether I wanted to stay or not: and while I was informed that it was not necessarily an order to come back home, there was a battleship waiting for me.

The audience roared with laughter, but Lindbergh's jest was a form of truth-telling: here at the very beginning of his fame he was ruefully in contention with its cost. The series of triumphant personal appearances that would make him a figure of awe and romance to millions of Americans had hardly begun, and already he was taking the measure of the misery he would feel by the time the series ended. It was more and more obvious that he had foreseen almost everything about his flight except its consequences. In Paris, he had resolved not to become an icon; in America, he would not become a prisoner. Within his chosen field of aviation, he would have to find the means of remaining his own man.

The welcome that Lindbergh was given in New York has never been rivaled. It lasted for four days and on every day there was an unbroken succession of parades, luncheons, dinners, and private and public receptions. On the morning of the first day, on the traditional drive up Broadway, a couple of tons of ticker tape and confetti were showered upon his motorcade from the windows of the skyscrapers in the financial district. At City Hall, Mayor James J. Walker gave a light-hearted oration ("Colonel Lindbergh, New York City is yours—I don't give it to you; you won it"), and in Central Park he was received and publicly praised by Governor Alfred E. Smith. That evening, a large dinner-dance in his honor was given at the great country house of a millionaire businessman named Clarence Mackay. The next morning, the New York Times devoted its first sixteen pages to Lindbergh; in the eyes of the editors, he was plainly the greatest single event in American history.

At one of the parties in New York, Raymond Orteig presented Lindbergh with a check for twenty-five thousand dollars and pronounced him officially the winner of the Orteig Prize. (The technicality of Lindbergh's not having obeyed the rules of the contest in regard to the period of time that was supposed to elapse between the receipt of his application and his take-off had been genially waived by Mr. Orteig.) From New York he flew to St. Louis, for two days of incessant celebrations, which he shared with the nine backers of the flight. In theory, the backers were entitled to a share in the prize as well as in the celebrations, but such was the general feeling about Lindbergh by this time that to have taken so much as a penny away from him would have struck the public as an act of gross presumption.

From St. Louis, Lindbergh made a quick flight to Dayton, Ohio, where he hoped to enjoy a quiet visit with Orville Wright. So many thousands of well-wishers turned up at Wright's house and clamored to see Lindbergh that Wright's gardens were soon trampled into dust and the house itself was threatened with serious damage. To placate the crowd, Wright persuaded Lindbergh to make a brief appearance on a balcony overlooking the front steps of the house, and the crowd eventually dispersed. Lindbergh had reason to recognize the truth of Alexander Hamilton's harsh dictum—"The people? The people, sir, is a great beast"—for again and again he found himself in greater danger from thousands of admiring strangers on the ground than he was from any natural or mechanical hazard that he was apt to encounter aloft.

Lindbergh returned to New York in late June, to start work on a book about the flight. The publishing house of G. P. Putnam's Sons had commissioned the book, and because it would have to be brought out as quickly as possible, in order to take advantage of Lindbergh's mounting fame, and because every moment of Lindbergh's time was thought to be already spoken for, the publishers assumed that the book would need

As Lindbergh lands at the Battery,
preparatory to the ride up Broadway.

Lindbergh riding uptown
with Mayor 'Jimmie' Walker.

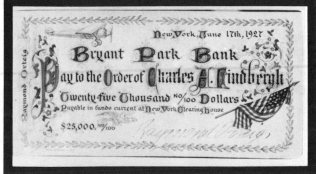

The Orteig Prize.

The traditional welcome of heroes to New York: a parade up Broadway to City Hall.

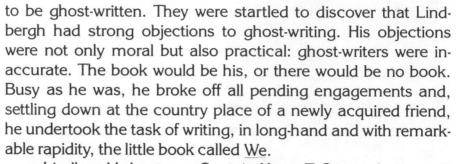

to be ghost-written. They were startled to discover that Lindbergh had strong objections to ghost-writing. His objections were not only moral but also practical: ghost-writers were inaccurate. The book would be his, or there would be no book. Busy as he was, he broke off all pending engagements and, settling down at the country place of a newly acquired friend, he undertook the task of writing, in long-hand and with remarkable rapidity, the little book called <u>We</u>.

Lindbergh's host was Captain Harry F. Guggenheim, and he recounts their meeting in his notes for the ''Autobiography of Values'':

> While I was at Curtiss Field before taking off for Paris, many influential people had come to see my plane. Among them were Harry Guggenheim and his wife, Carol. He was president of the Daniel Guggenheim Fund for the Promotion of Aeronautics, about which I had read in aviation magazines. After I showed them the <u>Spirit of St. Louis</u>, Guggenheim said, ''When you get back from your flight, look me up.'' Later, he told me he had not thought there was much chance of my getting back from such a flight. I had considered his invitation a gesture of politeness and dismissed it from my mind; but events thereafter brought us together often, first in the development of aviation, later in personal friendship.
>
> Harry Guggenheim had been a Navy aviator in World War I. He was a son of one of America's richest families. His grandfather Meyer Guggenheim emigrated to the United States from a Swiss ghetto in the mid-nineteenth century, started out as a peddler in Pennsylvania, and thereafter made his fortune in the mining business. Meyer's sons had augmented that fortune and they had strong feelings of gratitude to the country that had given them a freedom of action Jewish people were denied in Europe. As a result, the Guggenheims established various philanthropic foundations, endowed with tens of millions of dollars.

Harry Guggenheim had persuaded his father to give three million dollars to a fund, named for the father, that would foster an interest in flying; this was precisely what Lindbergh had it in mind to do, not by means of money but by the example of his life. Carol and Harry Guggenheim were some years older than Lindbergh and they proved to be sympathetic guides to the new world that he was entering—the world of the rich and powerful, with their great houses and, when they chose to exercise it, their enviable capacity for isolating themselves from the unnerving hubbub of New York. The Guggenheim estate, "Falaise," at Sands Point, Long Island, consisted of something over three hundred acres of fields, pastures, and woods, not unlike those of the Lindbergh "farm" back in Little Falls, with Long Island Sound taking the place of the Mississippi. The main house stood on a high bluff looking out over the Sound towards the Connecticut shore. (Many years later, the Lindbergh family would settle down in a big house in Darien, Connecticut, looking back across the Sound towards "Falaise." Lindbergh often said that he was unable to live long out of sight of water.)

"Falaise" provided Lindbergh with the privacy required to write his book and enjoy a comparatively normal existence. He was protected in that green fastness from exigent, hero-worshipping crowds and a press that pursued him even when he had no news to impart. Moreover, there was a horse-pasture on the property that served admirably as an air-strip, so Lindbergh could fly in and out at will. It was at "Falaise" that he took Anne Morrow up in a rented plane on the first of the three dates they had before they became engaged; few couples can ever have been brave enough—hopeful enough—to become engaged in greater ignorance of their natures. In later years, the Lindberghs often returned to "Falaise" and the Guggenheims always put them up in what became known in the family as the Lindbergh bedroom. "Falaise" is now a museum, and the bedroom, furnished just as it used to be, is open to the public.

Lindbergh took to the rich with an ease that chagrined some of his liberal admirers. Eastern millionaires, and especially Eastern millionaires who were bankers, had been his father's natural enemies, but he bore them no inherited grudge; he liked the Davisons and the Lamonts and the Morrows—all Morgan partners—to say nothing of the Morgans themselves. They were in fact kindly and pleasing people, who had the good manners to ignore his celebrity and who showed that they were genuinely glad to be in his company. For he <u>was</u> a most interesting young man and in the purity of his intentions

(Opposite, top) Triumphal return to St. Louis. (Bottom) Forest Park, St. Louis. The crowd has just caught sight of the *Spirit of St. Louis,* making its first appearance in the city since it had left in early May en route to New York and Paris.

Two rare eighteenth-century silver spheres, one terrestrial and the other celestial, presented to Lindbergh by William Randolph Hearst.

he struck them as a nonpareil. He was willing enough to get rich, but he would not allow himself to be wantonly exploited. Before the flight, he had endorsed certain products that he used on the flight—gas, oil, the Wright engine, the Waterman pen with which he kept his log—but most of the offers that had come to him since the flight he had been quick to reject. His total earnings in the twelve months following his flight probably amounted to something like half a million dollars. It is a sufficiently impressive sum; still more impressive is the fact that he earned it in the legitimate pursuit of his career as a champion of aviation. We, for example, was an immediate best seller; published in the late summer of 1927, it went through twenty-eight printings in the first six months and earned Lindbergh well over a hundred thousand dollars in royalties within that period.

Lindbergh might have earned several million dollars in the months after his return from Paris if he had been willing to exploit himself to the full. "When I arrived in New York," he wrote later, "I was deluged with tens of thousands of letters, telegrams, and phone calls. These contained many business propositions varying from a request that I become president of a manufacturing company to an offer of fifty thousand dollars for my signed endorsement of a cigarette. [Charles Curtis, of the United States Senate, was currently endorsing Lucky Strike cigarettes.] When I replied to the latter that I did not smoke, the company's representative said he would give me a package so I could speak truthfully and from experience." Gene Tunney, the heavyweight boxing champion of the world and a man second in fame only to Lindbergh himself, was quoted in a newspaper interview as saying that Lindbergh "ought to commercialize his stunt for every cent that's in it, for in a year from now he will be forgotten." Tunney was vociferously denounced as a cynic by rich and poor alike. In the first place, Lindbergh's flight wasn't a "stunt," in the second place, it was too heroic an act to be besmirched by commerce, and in the third place Lindbergh would never be forgotten. Rich and poor alike wished him to have money enough to make him independent, but not money enough to change his character.

# LINDBERGH ALONE

One rich man who responded charmingly, even tenderly, to Lindbergh was the publisher William Randolph Hearst, to whom history ordinarily gives few high marks for charm and tenderness. Lindbergh had refused an offer of a hundred thousand dollars for a lecture tour, but when Hearst offered him a movie contract with a minimum guarantee of half a million dollars, Lindbergh hesitated. Hearst assured him that the movie would be confined to aviation and would be filmed with dignity and taste. Lindbergh himself would play the leading role. Half a million dollars was more than thirty times what the Spirit of St. Louis and the flight to Paris had cost; it was also, Lindbergh calculated, more than he would have been able to earn in a whole lifetime as an air-mail pilot. The filming would require only a few months, after which he would be a man of independent means. The picture would contribute to the public interest in flying, so why shouldn't he accept the offer?

The difficulty was that Hearst's publishing empire, which extended from coast to coast and included magazines and radio stations as well as newspapers and movies, embodied values at the farthest possible remove from Lindbergh's.

> They seemed to me [he wrote later] sensational, inaccurate, and excessively occupied with the troubles and vices of mankind. I disliked most of the men I had met who represented him.
>
> Hearst suggested that I come and talk to him at his apartment in New York. I was as apprehensive as fascinated when I went there. It was a large and elaborately furnished place, full of paintings and antique articles, and dominated by a man of extraordinary character—tall, heavily built, with pale-blue eyes and a high-pitched voice. He welcomed me warmly and informally and handed me a motion-picture contract ready for signature. A paper worth half a million dollars, possibly twice that much, was in my fingers. I felt embarrassed, for I had already practically concluded that I would not take part in a motion picture—that I did not want to become a Hollywood actor even temporarily. Also I realized that my flight to Paris had placed me in a position from which I could do a great deal to accelerate aviation's progress during the months ahead, and I wanted to be free to devote my primary efforts to this end. Of course I had to make a living, and it seemed wise to set apart some extra

money while the opportunity was there; but I believed I could do this without extending my activities beyond my own profession. . . .

The old man—Hearst was sixty-four—and the young man gravely regarded each other. Rather than make an instant refusal, Lindbergh asked if he might have a night in which to think the matter over. Hearst agreed to let him do so. The next evening, Lindbergh returned and began diffidently to explain his reasons for not wishing to sign the contract. Hearst made no effort to change Lindbergh's mind. He said pleasantly, "Just tear it up and throw it in the fire." The suggestion caused Lindbergh to feel even more embarrassed than he had been on the previous evening. He started to hand the contract back to him, with profuse thanks. Hearst said, "No, if you don't want to make a picture, tear it up and throw it away."

Lindbergh tore the contract in half and tossed it into the fireplace near which he and Hearst were standing. Hearst watched with what Lindbergh took to be mingled astonishment and amusement. Neither of them said another word about movies. Lindbergh talked for a time about his flight and about aviation in general. He admired two antique silver globes—one celestial, one terrestrial—that were standing on a table. After a few more minutes, the two men shook hands and said good-bye.

The next day a messenger arrived at the apartment in which Lindbergh was staying and handed him a present from Hearst—the two antique silver globes. Lindbergh was told afterwards that they were valued at more than forty thousand dollars. Today, along with many thousands of other gifts received by Lindbergh after the flight, the globes are in the collection of the Missouri Historical Society, in St. Louis. The collection, donated by Lindbergh in 1929, is estimated to be worth $300,000.

Lindbergh's flight is something rare in history: an event as simple and perfect in execution as it was in plan. It had the elegance of any problem that has been solved with the minimum of means; looking back on it, we can study it as we might study one or another of Hearst's silver globes, picking it up and turning it round in the light and observing that it is all of a piece, all without flaw. The simplicity and perfection of the flight were thanks in large part to the fact that it was the handiwork of a single man; the help that Lindbergh got from others, important as it was, had been at his bidding and under his direction. Though the adventure was capable of being shared vicariously by millions, it had been experienced by him alone. And that aloneness added a hint of the legendary, even of the mysterious, to an event that might otherwise have seemed too straightforward to hold our interest, once the inevitable advances of technology had caused it to be surpassed. But more important than the flight was the maker of the flight; from the beginning, it was plain that no subsequent transatlantic adventure could diminish the scale or darken the lustre of Lindbergh's solitary pioneering one, for there loomed the flier himself, from youth into age a man tirelessly bent upon winning greatness.

Several of Lindbergh's former rivals for the Orteig Prize were not long in following him across the Atlantic. Within two weeks of Lindbergh's touching down at Le Bourget, Chamberlin and Levine, in their Bellanca-designed Columbia, flew the Atlantic to Eisleben, Germany, exceeding Lindbergh's record for long-distance flying by five hundred miles. And three weeks after the Columbia flight, Commander Byrd and his crew, in their tri-motored Fokker, the America, after a stormy crossing made a forced landing off the French coast. The flights aroused a great deal of excitement, but they were far from having been perfectly carried out. Chamberlin and Levine had set forth from New York with no other destination in mind than "somewhere in Europe." Having decided when they reached the continent to try for Rome, they were obliged to settle instead for little, unknown Eisleben. They landed bumpily in a swamp outside the town, the plane flipped up on its nose, and

Price Studio 1928

Landing at Val Buena Airport, Mexico City, in December, 1927.

Lindbergh with Gene Tunney and the artist
Charles Baskerville, in Baskerville's New York
studio.

both passengers were in danger of serious injury. Byrd and his crew plunged into the sea near the little town of Ver-sur-Mer and came close to being killed. Both flights proved that the Atlantic was indeed capable of being crossed by air, but they also made it obvious that many years would pass before such flights would become a commercial commonplace.

Meanwhile, Lindbergh was making plans for a new ad-venture: one that disguised its difficulty behind its avowed pur-pose, which was to demonstrate the safety and practicality of air travel throughout the States. While he had been engaged in writing <u>We</u>, he had received hundreds of requests for personal appearances. Now it occurred to him that he could honor those requests and, at the same time, assume a role that he believed in and that the success of his Paris flight had more or less imposed on him—the role of chief spokesman for the new world of commercial aviation. In behalf of that cause, he would undertake a tour of cities from coast to coast, demonstrating that when it came to maintaining regular schedules planes were already approaching the reliability of trains and other methods of surface transportation (a demonstration that, at the time, probably no one but Lindbergh was capable of mak-ing). Lindbergh's friend Guggenheim saw the tour as an ideal project for the Fund for the Promotion of Aeronautics. The Fund would gladly underwrite the cost of the tour and would pay Lindbergh a fee of fifty thousand dollars; it would also be willing to share sponsorship of the tour with the United States-Department of Commerce, which, under Secretary Herbert C. Hoover, was trying to stimulate an interest in the manufacture of more planes and the construction of more airports.

Starting in July and ending in October, Lindbergh flew well over twenty-two thousand miles in two hundred and sixty flying hours. He made scheduled stops in eighty-two cities and flew over and dropped messages on innumerable other cities at designated hours. He devoted a hundred and forty-seven speeches to the general topic of aviation. As usual, he had little to say about himself and in interviews he refused to answer any personal questions; whenever he was asked whether he pre-ferred blondes or brunettes, he would say curtly, "What has

Posing with Ambassador Dwight W. Morrow, Mrs. Morrow, and their daughter Constance, at the United States Embassy in Mexico City.

The *Spirit of St. Louis* being delivered to the Smithsonian, in Washington, D.C., on May 12, 1928.

that to do with aviation?" He was the guest of honor at sixty-nine dinners and was driven nearly thirteen hundred miles in parades. "I inspected sites for airports," he wrote long afterwards, "talked to engineers and politicians, and tried to convince everyone who would listen that aviation had a brilliant future, in which America should lead."

A total of thirty million people were estimated to have seen Lindbergh and the <u>Spirit of St. Louis</u> in the course of the tour, and there was no doubt whatever that the tour greatly increased the public's interest in both air travel and air-mail. The Post Office had been carrying less than a hundred thousand pounds of air-mail in April and by autumn it was carrying almost a hundred and fifty thousand pounds. According to Postmaster General New, this large increase was thanks entirely to Lindbergh. Remembering the times when the leather-and-canvas air-mail sacks he was carrying from St. Louis to Chicago weighed more than the correspondence they contained, Lindbergh could not fail to be pleased. He must also have been pleased to know that many of the air-mail letters crisscrossing the United States that summer bore a stamp depicting him and his plane on their way to Paris. He was the first living American ever to have been so honored.

Lindbergh had still another reason to be pleased—the tour had provided him with a new sort of acquaintanceship with his country. From boyhood, he had been preoccupied with exploring as much of it as he could. He had taken a large-scale map belonging to his father and on it from year to year, in different colors, had traced his various expeditions, whether by bicycle, motorcycle, automobile, boat, or, finally, plane. Long before the flight to Paris, he had come to know far more of America than most of his contemporaries, from Florida to California and from Texas north to the Canadian border. With a note of personal pride rare in his writings, in the nineteen-sixties he set down his lyrical recollection of what must often have been, in other respects, an exhausting ordeal:

> That tour let me know my country as no man had ever known it before. When I returned to New York in October, the United States was represented by a new image in my mind. In-

stead of outlines on a paper map, I saw New England's valleys dotted by white villages, the crystal waters of Michigan's great lakes, Arizona's pastel deserts, Georgia's red cotton fields, the cascades and deep forests of the Oregon northwest. I saw three great mountain ranges running north and south: the Appalachians, the Rockies, the Sierras—walls of a continent, holding rivers, warning off oceans. I saw waves foaming on the rocks of Maine, cloud layers pressing against Washington's Olympics. I saw California's "Golden Gate," Louisiana's delta, Florida's wide sand beaches hundreds of miles in length.

There were intimacies, too, detailed points of matter and of life. I circled a glacial lake in the high Sierras, almost inaccessible by foot, and saw its clear water like the air above; I saw its gray-rock bottom; I saw wild horses galloping over Oklahoma badlands; I saw a skiff-filled harbor in New Hampshire, with fishermen standing at their nets and looking up; I dived into Death Valley, its hot sands ten feet below my wheels; I saw, wedged down between sun-seared mountains, a village of Indian teepees apparently deserted except for one teepee that brought all the rest to life, for stuck in its triangular entrance was a fat squaw struggling to take cover from my wings.

By bad luck, on the first day of the tour Lindbergh was unable to land at Portland, Maine, because the airport was fogged in. With that single exception, he appeared over every city on his itinerary within a minute or two—often within a few seconds—of the time previously announced for his arrival.

This formidable demonstration of flying skill was matched by the non-stop flight he made in December between Washington, D.C., and Mexico City, which proved in some respects more difficult and no less dangerous than the flight to Paris. Dwight W. Morrow, the United States Ambassador to Mexico, was chairman of a committee appointed by President Coolidge to investigate the state of American aviation. Morrow, who had met Lindbergh in Washington, invited him to express his views at a conference being held at Morrow's apartment in New York. Afterwards, Morrow invited Lindbergh to fly to Mexico on a good-will visit. "The Ambassador's invitation gave me an opportunity to accomplish several objectives on a single flight," Lindbergh wrote in his "Autobiography of Values." "In

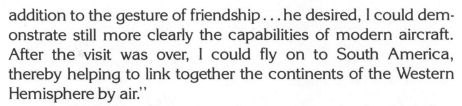

addition to the gesture of friendship...he desired, I could demonstrate still more clearly the capabilities of modern aircraft. After the visit was over, I could fly on to South America, thereby helping to link together the continents of the Western Hemisphere by air."

Ambassador Morrow was upset when he learned that Lindbergh intended to fly non-stop to Mexico. He had expected the journey to be made in easy stages, as an extension of Lindbergh's recent tour of the States. He protested that he didn't want Lindbergh to do anything hazardous on his behalf, and Lindbergh smilingly rejoined that the Ambassador was to stop worrying and leave the flying problems to him. He would fly between the two capitals in order to give the flight political significance and to heighten its effect on Congressmen. Moreover, instead of selecting the best possible conditions, as he had done for the Paris flight—planning it for the short nights of spring and waiting for favorable weather—he would fly through the lengthy darkness of a December night. He would announce the time of his arrival in Mexico City several days in advance and would attempt to hold to schedule regardless of wind, fog, or storm, as though he were on a routine mail flight between St. Louis and Chicago.

Lindbergh took off at twenty-two minutes past noon on December 13, 1927, from Bolling Field, in Washington, D.C. He had already revealed his intention of arriving at Valbuena Airport, in Mexico City, at precisely noon on the following day. He had calculated that the distance between Washington and Mexico City was twenty-one hundred miles, which was fifteen hundred miles less than the distance between New York and Paris. This meant that the Spirit of St. Louis could afford to carry a proportionately smaller amount of gasoline than it had carried on May 20 and should have much less trouble taking off. Lindbergh had even permitted himself the luxury of adding extra gear to the emergency equipment in the fuselage behind his cockpit—a rifle, a machete, and some tropical medicines. Still, heavy rains had been drenching Washington and Bolling Field had no paved runways for use in bad weather. On the morning of December 13, Lindbergh walked back and forth over the section of the field that the direction of the wind obliged him to use. He kicked his heels into the sod to test its firmness, hunted for paths between deep pools of water, and made up his mind about the point at which he would either cut the throttle or commit himself to taking off.

The account of the take-off in the New York Times is a fair specimen of how Lindbergh was written about in the press in those days. It is charged with an adulation so excessive that one sees that it was bound sooner or later to turn skeptical, if not vindictive. One also sees that it was bound to repel Lindbergh:

> Intent, cool, clear-eyed and clear-headed, under conditions requiring supreme moral and physical courage and consummate skill, America's young viking of the air lifted his gray plane from a hummocky, soggy, puddle-bespattered morass into an underhanging fringe of threatening mists just before noon today, pointed its nose southwestward, and was off again on a new, hazardous adventure to a foreign land—perhaps to other and more distant lands—personifying again in the hearts of his people their unofficial ambassador of good will....

The one hard fact in that lead—the time of take-off—the reporter for the Times, managed to get wrong, and Lindbergh would not have been surprised. He flew all day south over Virginia, the Carolinas, and Georgia, dodging heavy squalls, and then on through the night over Alabama, Mississippi, and Louisiana. Spotting the shore of the Gulf of Mexico below him in the dark, he followed it over Texas until, at about nine in the morning, he reached Tampico, Mexico. There the clouds were so low that he had to climb steeply to get above them; finding a saddle in the mountains west of Tampico, he flew on into the high, sun-baked Valley of Mexico. The squalls and fog and dense clouds were behind him. The sky was blue and the visibility unlimited; he assumed that he had endured the worst of the flight and that he would easily reach the Valbuena Airport by noon. And then to his astonishment he made an unpleasant discovery: he was lost. For perhaps the second or third time in his life, he hadn't the slightest notion of where he was.

The best maps of Mexico that Lindbergh had been able to

obtain in the States showed few details—straightish black lines, representing railroads, occasionally crossed wavy blue lines, representing rivers, but looking back and forth between the maps on his knees and the terrain below him he could make nothing match. He followed a railroad westward, hoping that it would intersect with another railroad and thereby form an angle that he could recognize. No such angle ever appeared. Next, he tried a method that he had commonly employed in his barnstorming days. Strung out along the railroad line at infrequent intervals were villages and hamlets, each of them with a railroad station. Back in the States, every such station would have affixed to its end walls black-painted signs giving the name of the town. He had often "shot" such stations in order to check on the correctness of his route; now he began to "shoot" the little Mexican stations, dropping to within fifty feet of the ground in order to do so. He saw a sign, "Caballeros," but he could find no town of that name printed on the map. Another town and again the sign "Caballeros." And again and then again, maddeningly. He had been over twenty-five hours without sleep and his responses were slowing down; at last it dawned on him that the word on the signs indicated not the name of the town but the presence of toilet facilities.

So there he was, lost in broad daylight, in perfect flying weather, and the time at which he had promised to arrive in Mexico City was long since past. The Ambassador would be on the field waiting to greet him and no doubt there would be a sizeable crowd as well. And where was the self-confident young pilot who had told the Ambassador not to worry—just to leave the flying problems to him? "Shooting" men's rooms in no man's land! He opened the throttle and climbed to fourteen thousand feet; at that height he could see clearly for up to fifty miles. In the distance he observed what appeared to be a fairly large city. He banked toward it and as he lost altitude he made out in huge letters on a windowless wall the name "Hotel Toluca." He looked on the map—yes, there was a city by that name, about thirty-five miles west and south of Mexico City. He raced at top speed for the capital.

# LINDBERGH ALONE

Within twenty minutes, he had landed at the Valbuena Airport. He was two hours and forty minutes late and he was profoundly embarrassed. (He was also aware of the humor of the situation. In his account of the flight, which appears as a dispatch to the New York _Times_, he wrote, "Something went wrong, and it must have been me.") Ambassador Morrow was there to greet him—indeed, he had been waiting to greet him for several hours, having taken care to reach the airport early. Pacing up and down, he had been increasingly distracted as the minutes passed with no sign of his ever-punctual young friend; until word reached the airport that Lindbergh had been sighted over Toluca, he had been sure that some terrible accident must have befallen him and he had been ready to hold himself to blame.

Not only Ambassador Morrow was waiting at Valbuena—so was the President of Mexico, Plutarco Calles, along with a crowd estimated at a hundred and fifty thousand people. In the general relief at Lindbergh's safe arrival, nobody appears to have objected to his tardiness. Perhaps it was a case of tardiness being less of a sin to Mexicans than it was to time-haunted Yankees like Morrow and Lindbergh. In any event, his presence in the capital was celebrated for six consecutive days, in what was said to be the greatest fiesta ever held in Mexico in honor of a foreigner. Presidents Coolidge and Calles both issued formal statements, thanking Lindbergh for helping to foster good relations between the two countries.

During the next six weeks, Lindbergh flew to fourteen Latin-American countries, as well as to the Canal Zone, being welcomed everywhere not as an unheralded boy but as some sort of divine apparition dropping benignly out of the skies. On his twenty-sixth birthday, he flew from Puerto Rico to Santo Domingo; by then, he was already making plans to bring his "public" life to an end. He had had enough of being an apparition, a hero, a Viking, a lone eagle. He would settle down to a business career in aviation. He would marry and have children (the only child had always contemplated having a large family). He would walk through the streets unnoticed. And the sign and proof of his intention to eschew all future fame was his de-

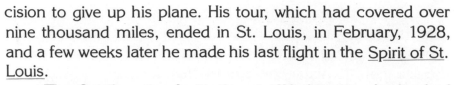

cision to give up his plane. His tour, which had covered over nine thousand miles, ended in St. Louis, in February, 1928, and a few weeks later he made his last flight in the <u>Spirit of St. Louis</u>.

The Smithsonian Institution, in Washington, had asked for the plane, in order to put in on permanent exhibition next to the Wright Brothers' <u>Kitty Hawk</u>. Lindbergh loved flying the <u>Spirit of St. Louis</u>, and he would be sorry never to be able to fly it again, but he had been in constant apprehension of its being torn to pieces by admiring crowds. Again and again on the Latin-American trip both he and the plane had been in jeopardy. To make matters worse, the plane itself had threatened to prove murderous. Like most planes of that day, it had no brakes and was extremely difficult to maneuver on the ground. Crowds invariably rushed up to the plane while its propeller was still spinning. Lindbergh, who had once seen a man chopped in two by a propeller, feared that the <u>Spirit of St. Louis</u> might some day be blamed for causing a similar accident. In the air, it was as innocent as it was beautiful, and precious to him beyond measure, but on the ground it became a dangerous weapon. For the plane's sake, as well as for the sake of his future, he flew from St. Louis to Washington on April 30, 1928, and turned the <u>Spirit of St. Louis</u> over to officials of the Smithsonian. Many times during most of the next half-century, he would stroll into the Smithsonian and with a hat shadowing his face, at a distance from any crowd, he would stare up at the little plane, hanging alone in space.

**A**t that moment in 1928, less than a year after he had passed from obscurity to unprecedented fame, almost two-thirds of Lindbergh's life lay before him. He was thought of as a boy, and in some respects he <u>was</u> a boy, but in other respects he had been a man since early childhood. He had faced choices and made decisions as an adult does, always inside that framework of freedom with responsibility which his father and mother had passed on to him as an inheritance from their unusually free and responsible parents. "He exercises the most sense for one of his age that I have ever taken notice of," C.A. had written to Evangeline, in 1922. "I would like to be out in the wild with him for two weeks again, like when we were up the Mississippi River. Kind of a strange feeling comes over one [to see] these once little ones climbing up to full manhood—stronger even than the parents. Such is the world. I miss his boy days, but he takes his turn the same as we did ours. You need not worry about him."

For Lindbergh, taking his turn was nearly always the equivalent of taking charge, and there can be little doubt that when he left his plane in the custody of the Smithsonian he believed himself to be announcing a new and different phase of his career. From his first days in Paris, he had been aware that he was doomed to become a public figure; nevertheless, he supposed that he would be able to remain to some extent a private figure as well and that the location and height of the barrier between his public and private self would be fixed by him and not by others. With the Latin-American tour, he had earned the right to retire behind that barrier and let his fame go hang. Up to that moment, he had behaved largely as his elders—Herrick, Coolidge, Morrow, those innumerable proud surrogate fathers—had wished him to behave, and yet it was true that he had done nothing against his will. If most of the activities in which he had been taking part were, as he said later, "intellectually, intuitively, and sensually distasteful to me," he had understood their purposes and had consented to them. Now it was over: the time had come to put a stop to tours and crowds.

Lindbergh assumed that when he announced a return to

wight W. Morrow campaigning for the U.S. Senate.

After a dead-stick landing, at the Homer Aitkens' farm, in Oklahoma, in 1928.

private life his fame would begin to subside as spontaneously as it had arisen. Nor was he naïve or disingenuous in making this assumption. We look back on those years and we see clearly enough that his fame didn't diminish—that, on the contrary, for a long while it continued to increase—and the more skeptical among us would argue that Lindbergh was aware from the beginning that his life would take the course it did and that all his protestations were but the sly feints of a man who pursues fame by affecting to run away from it. The less skeptical among us would argue that the facts of American history are otherwise and that they are on Lindbergh's side.

We have a tradition in this country of creating famous figures overnight, using them up, and then discarding them. It is a tradition so well established that journalists practice as a dependable source of income the writing of articles that ask, in one guise or another, "Where are they now?" The New Yorker, which in its early years published a number of articles under that heading, in the first months after Lindbergh's flight preoccupied itself not with the remarkable nature of his achievement but with questions about how long his fame would last and how much money he would be able to squeeze out of it before it faded. If the subtlest journalistic opinion of the day never doubted that his fame was transitory, then Lindbergh did well to agree with that opinion and attempt to act on it. Unfortunately, the opinion was wrong and he acted on it in vain. So far from having used him up, the public wanted more of him, and yet more, and so an unseemly tug of war began between the press and him, which ended only with his death.

The reporters' point of view was then, as it is now, the conventional one: that it is they who decide what is news and what is not. Moreover (though this they say less loudly), anybody they write about is in part their invention and therefore belongs to them and is answerable to them on their terms. Lindbergh's point of view was that the reporters never troubled to find out who he was and that the succession of Lindberghs they invented, whether favorable or unfavorable, were travesties. He—the authentic Lindbergh—volunteered to sit down with reporters and draw up a set of rules, to which they and he would promise to comply. He would keep them informed at all times of the events of his professional life; they would refrain from seeking out and publishing the events of his private life. In 1928, that seemed to him a possible solution to the problem. The reporters jeered at him behind his back. Neither they nor the public which read their dispatches had more than a cursory interest in his professional life. The greatest flier in the world would be busy over the next few years laying out commercial air-routes within the United States and commercial air-routes between the United States and other continents, and from time to time he would be flying faster, or higher, or longer than any other human being had ever flown, and those feats were as nothing compared to the scoops, true or false, that sold papers. Again and again the black headlines would blazon forth a fiction about his latest girl friend, his latest illness, his latest accident, his latest death.

The young man striving to bid good-bye to fame was to have many bright passages in his life and many dark ones. It is distressing to observe that, whether the passages were dark or bright, the press at large would invariably behave in regard to them with the same insolent outrageousness. The happiest event of Lindbergh's life was certainly his falling in love with and marrying Anne Morrow, but their courtship and honeymoon were made harrowing by reporters who pursued them night and day, by boat, plane, and car, and whose constantly reiterated question to Lindbergh, whenever they succeeded in running him to earth over the next few months, was, "What about it, Lindy? She pregnant?" The saddest event in Lindbergh's life was the kidnapping and murder, in 1932, of his infant son and namesake. The press turned the event into a sideshow ("Read all about it! Biggest story of the century!"), and no sooner was the child's body found than a couple of newspaper photographers broke into the morgue in Trenton in an attempt to prise open the little coffin and take a photograph of the remains.

When the Lindberghs' second son, Jon, was born, he had to be guarded around the clock not only from potential kidnappers and murderers—scores of threatening letters were received after his birth—but also from reporters and newsreel and still photographers, who attempted to bribe the servants and deliverymen into taking his picture and who concealed themselves in the backs of moving vans and other portable hiding places in order to spy on him. Their hope was to get a close-up that could be sold to editors and featured on the front page of no telling how many hundreds of papers from coast to coast—the very picture that the Lindberghs with good reason were bending every effort not to have taken. Once, a car in which Jon was being driven to kindergarten was forced up onto the curb by another car; out jumped some photographers, who thrust their cameras full in the face of the frightened child. There were many such incidents, and in 1935 the Lindberghs felt obliged to leave the United States altogether, taking up residence in a secluded house in the English countryside, where (so they had been correctly informed) the press and the public would leave them quite alone.

Flying for Lindbergh had long since ceased to be an end in itself and had become a means to many ends. For example, it enabled his wife and him to undertake a journey of aerial exploration in the American Southwest, where they photographed ancient Indian cave-dwellings, and a journey into the jungles of Guatemala, where in the company of archeologists from the Carnegie Institution they mapped and studied Mayan ruins. Already Lindbergh was beginning to be haunted by the mystery of man's long past; the schoolboy impatient with books was making himself into a scholar of pre-history. The Lindberghs' long over-ocean flights on behalf of Pan Am are important enough in the annals of commercial aviation, but they have a measure of importance in the annals of American writing as well: they provided the occasion for two best-selling books by Anne Lindbergh—North to the Orient and Listen! the Wind—which read as well in the seventies as they did in the thirties. (Her exquisite short novel The Steep Ascent was also prompted by one of their flights.) In his introduction to Listen! the Wind, Lindbergh described their nearly six-months-long series of flights as being about "a period of aviation which is now gone, but which was probably more interesting than any the future will bring." He foresaw that the planes of the present day would outwit most of the natural hazards against which he and his wife had had to contend; the more sophisticated the technology of flight, the less emotion it would be capable of evoking.

Planes would lose their interest, but there might be other forms of flight in store for man. Lindbergh was among the first to have his imagination kindled by the idea of rockets. Having learned by chance of some experiments in liquid-fuel rocketry being carried out by an obscure professor named Robert H. Goddard, who taught at Clark University, in Worcester, Massachusetts, Lindbergh with characteristic spontaneity immediately got in touch with Goddard, visited with him in Worcester, and came away from their meeting convinced of the practicality of Goddard's experiments. What Goddard needed was money enough to carry out on a comparatively large scale notions that for lack of money had so far remained largely on paper. Lindbergh appealed to his friends the Guggenheims, who consented to back Goddard. As simply and pleasingly as that, the means of opening up an entirely new world of flight were found; Goddard built an experimental rocket station near Roswell, New Mexico, and Lindbergh often joined him there, observing the first uncertain steps by which we were eventually to catapult ourselves into outer space, land on the moon, and set scientific equipment gently down upon the rocky plains of Mars.

Ever since 1930, Lindbergh had been adding to his brilliant career in aviation a scarcely less brilliant career as a medical technician. In close collaboration with Dr. Alexis Carrel, at the Rockefeller Institute for Medical Research, in New York City, he devoted several years to the development of a pump for perfusing living organs. Carrel and Lindbergh made the first announcement of the pump in the magazine Science, in 1935, and three years later they jointly published a book, The Culture of Organs. Carrel had a dazzling, wayward mind, full of cranky notions that he would often improvise highly improbable "scientific" evidence for. Like Lindbergh, he was both exceptionally adept with his hands—the story went that he

(Opposite, top) July, 1929. Mary Pickford has just christened a Ford trimotor plane, The City of Los Angeles, at the start of the first regularly scheduled coast-to-coast air service. (Opposite, bottom) Lindbergh with Juan T. Trippe, President of Pan American Airlines. The time is September, 1929, and Charles and Anne Lindbergh are inaugurating air-mail service to Trinidad and Surinam with an amphibian Sikorsky S-38.

Landing at Roosevelt Field after a record-breaking flight from the West Coast.

The Lindberghs exploring a pueblo in the American Southwest. The time is 1929.

Charles A. Lindbergh, Jr., celebrating his first birthday.

could tie a knot with two fingers of one hand inside an ordinary small match-box—and exceptionally preoccupied with the nature of the unconscious mind. He had a tendency to exaggerate his accomplishments: a failing that Lindbergh never shared and that, surprisingly, he was willing to forgive in Carrel, perhaps because he looked up to him as the most gifted man he had ever met. In <u>The Culture of Organs</u>, Carrel boldly foresaw the day when "organs removed from the human body, in the course of an operation or soon after death, could be revived in the Lindbergh pump and made to function again when perfused with an artificial fluid." (The Lindbergh pump is still in use, in a different form and on a far smaller scale than Carrel predicted.)

Carrel was some thirty years older than Lindbergh and he had a profound effect upon the younger man's intellectual development. Disciplined as a surgeon, undisciplined as a thinker, he enjoyed bequeathing, as if to the son he never had, the legacy of a lifetime of unbridled speculation. "He believed in the supernatural realm," Lindbergh wrote. "He was always searching for bridges between the physical and the mystical. [How Carrel must have relished Lindbergh's description of his encounter with ghosts out over the stormy Atlantic!] He studied developments in the new field of psychosomatic medicine, listened intently to accounts of mental telepathy and clairvoyance, and was convinced of the efficacy of prayer."

In 1938, the Lindberghs gave up their house in England. With Jon and a new baby, their third son, whom they had christened Land Morrow, they moved to a tiny island called Illiec, off the coast of Brittany. It was only a few minutes by boat or, when the tide was low, on foot to the somewhat larger island of St. Gildas, where Carrel and his wife made their summer home. The composer Ambroise Thomas had owned Illiec in the late nineteenth century and had built a substantial stone manor house there. Living conditions were primitive and consequently very much to Lindbergh's taste. Illiec, he said, was second only to the farm at Little Falls as the most beautiful place he had ever lived in; he felt primordial forces lingering among the wizened, wind-wracked trees and he rejoiced at the great storms that would send sea-boulders flying over their stout slate rooftops. He and Carrel worked and talked together for long hours, either in a makeshift laboratory in the barn at St. Gildas or lying out on the rocks that guarded the island against the sea.

That life, pleasant and promising as it was, was soon to be interrupted by the Second World War. In 1939, the Lindberghs reluctantly abandoned Illiec and returned to the United States, where they rented a country place at Lloyd Neck, on Long Island. It was from there that Lindbergh, fully aware of what the cost to Anne and him would be, embarked on still another career—one that took from him most of his popularity without markedly diminishing his fame. At first on his own and then under the auspices of the America First Committee, he argued vehemently against America's entry into the war. This was one of the darkest passages of his life, not least because it meant the surrender of the privacy that he had struggled for so many years to achieve. He was again out among crowds, again in banner headlines, but now there was rancor in the air instead of joy. He heard boos and hisses as well as cheers and in the press he was more often denounced than acclaimed. In the course of an acrimonious running debate with the Roosevelt Administration, he felt obliged to resign his commission as a Colonel in the U.S. Army Air Corps. It was a high price to pay for what he saw as a citizen's right to free speech, but he had, he said, no choice in the matter; with his father's stoicism, he went on speaking his mind.

Lindbergh's career as a polemicist was ended by Pearl Harbor.

On the following day, he issued a statement through the America First Committee:

> We have been stepping closer to war for many months. Now it has come and we must meet it as united Americans regardless of our attitude in the past toward the policy our government has followed. Whether or not that policy has been wise, our country has been attacked by force of arms and by force of arms we must retaliate. Our own defenses and our own military position have already been neglected too long. We must now turn every effort to building up the greatest and most efficient

The Island of Illiec, off the French coast, which the Lindberghs purchased in 1938. It was close to a larger island, St. Gildas, where the Lindberghs' close friends Dr. and Mrs. Alexis Carrel spent their summers.

Lindbergh flying in England, in the sporty little Mohawk that he had had built according to his specifications.

Army, Navy, and Air Force in the world. When American soldiers go to war, it must be with the best equipment that modern skill can design and that modern industry can build.

Lindbergh was eager to become one of the first of those American soldiers on their way to war. He volunteered his services to the Air Corps, and it was conveyed to him that if the White House were to permit his commission to be restored to him, he must first publicly admit that he had been wrong. Lindbergh of course refused. His contribution to the war effort would have to be made as a civilian. It was galling, but his pride was intact. The dark passage that had lasted so long was beginning to brighten. Though he was no longer young, he was still far younger than his years. Soon he would be in the air again, doing what he was better fitted to do than any other man on earth.

Sooner than we expect (and sometimes sooner than we are ready for it) our lives begin to curve back upon themselves. Our mere daily busy-ness increases and we have the air of being more and more deeply implicated in the affairs of the world, but it is not so; consciously or unconsciously, in the turbulence of the middle years we are drawing away from the world and setting a fixed distance between its bounds and ours. After the war, Lindbergh shouldered a score of tasks, some of them for the Air Force, others for commercial aviation, still others for one or another of the philanthropies in which he took an increasing interest. He worked hard and traveled often, but at last, and for the first time in their married lives, the Lindberghs had a fixed point of departure and return—their country place in Darien. There they had come into possession of one of the few certain blessings: the merriment and distraction of a big old house filled with handsome, energetic children. There were three boys—Jon, Land, and Scott—and two girls—Anne and Reeve. Lindbergh sought to impose a discipline on the children's healthy unruliness, not always as successfully as he recalled his father's having been able to impose a similar discipline on him, in the house at Little Falls. Fatherhood was an art, like any other, and took time to learn.

The children grew up and scattered and married and the first of the grandchildren began to arrive. All his life, Lindbergh had been haunted by the way in which the generations of a family are able to bind themselves together through time; now he thought of his grandmother, who had known many people born in the eighteenth century, and of his grandchildren, who would live well into the twenty-first century, and he saw that he served as a bridge between them—in effect, a bridge that spanned four centuries. He wished that there were more sheer volume of information that could be carried back and forth across that bridge. He would do his best to see that nothing of value was lost; it was for that reason among others that he was accumulating the vast manuscript of his autobiography. He would tell his grandchildren stories, as his grandmother has told them to him. Some of them were fine stories for children, because they contained just the right mixture of the frightening and the bizarre. He would tell them, for example, the story of how his grandfather August, having had his arm amputated, asked that it be brought to him in its pine box. Old August shook the lifeless fingers at the end of the amputated arm and said slowly, in broken English, "You have been a good friend to me for fifty years. But you can't be with me any more. So good-by. Good-by, my friend."

There were other stories. One of the great adventures of his childhood had been the journey with his father along the headwaters of the Mississippi. He had kept an extensive diary of the trip, and his children and grandchildren would read it some day at their leisure; it might be that the writing—at any rate, the punctuation and spelling—left something to be desired, but he had no reason to be ashamed of the diary's narrative drive:

> ...it started raining again and to make it worse we came to a dam that was broken we had to unload all the stuff and lower the boat down with roaps it was raining all the time when we got the boat down to the worst part of the sloose she drew about 3 pailfuls of water in her first. To cap that we had to draw the boat over a foot bridge or boom stick we were pretty wet but a man by the name of Peterson happened to come down to fish he helped us with that and with the portaging of the stuff we had to make three trips of about 150 to 200 yards he said we could stay at his house overnight which we were very glad to accept we had to go through some rapids and over a foot bridge where his house was it was fun going through the rapids he had to take down part of the railing on the bridge and we had to take out the big box but we made it it was still drizzely and we put all of the stuff from the boat but what we had to take with us on some logs and covered them over with a bug proof tent to keep them from getting wet then we followed Peterson to the house it was very clean we had a cup of coffee and Father took some saying that it was the first time in four years but he had some last year in the auto trip saying the same thing.

Almost forty years after the Paris flight, Lindbergh flew over to Ireland and made his way for the first time down the coast from Shannon Airport to Dingle Bay, his point of landfall. He met an old shepherd out on the hills above the bay. "Wasn't this where Lindbergh flew over?" he asked him.

# LINDBERGH ALONE

"Aye," said the shepherd. "And did you happen to see him?" Lindbergh asked. The shepherd gave him a crestfallen look; after all the years, it was evidently still a sore point with him. "Do you know, I didn't? 'Twas all fog on the hills that day. But I heard him go over. I did that, now. I stood here listening."

Lindbergh never told the shepherd who he was. One imagines how happy the old man would have been, coming into his pub that night and working his way slowly, slowly into an account of the astonishing good fortune that had befallen him that day. Lindbergh! As close as this pint! But by that time Lindbergh liked keeping the secret of his identity; he had gained the anonymity of age and he would not lightly put it aside.

The children themselves were the occasions for stories. It was Land who, as a child in school, was asked by one of his classmates, "Didn't your father discover America?" Land replied, "Yes, and he flew across the ocean, too." Once Lindbergh and Reeve, aged 10, shared an adventure that was well worth preserving in the family archives. They had driven from Darien over to the Danbury airport, where Lindbergh had rented a plane. They had been in the air for only a few minutes when the plane's engine suddenly went dead; Lindbergh guessed afterward that the carburetor had iced up. Reeve saw that the propeller had stopped revolving and she asked in a calm voice, "Father, are we going to have an accident?" Lindbergh replied with equal calm, "I don't know."

The plane had not been very high when the engine failed. Lindbergh had lost much of the little altitude the plane had by diving it in an attempt to start the engine. They were over rocky Connecticut hills, heavily wooded. There was only one place where Lindbergh had a chance of landing the plane without cracking it up—a small hillside pasture, surrounded by trees, and with a number of boulders scattered over its surface. He would have to land uphill, regardless of the wind, but first he would have to glide through a gap between the trees at the lower end of the pasture—a gap that was not as wide as the wingspan of the plane. That meant that he must finish his glide in a side-slip, with the wings of the plane canted up to fit between the trees. The hillside was steep and the plane had brakes; they made a perfect landing. Since the pasture wasn't big enough to allow for a take-off, a day or so later the plane had to be disassembled and hauled back to the airport in a truck.

Reeve hadn't shown the slightest trace of nervousness during the course of her father's difficult maneuvering. It turned out that she had been waiting patiently for the correct answer to her question. He was Charles A. Lindbergh, after all—the greatest flier in the world. When she asked him, "Father, are we going to have an accident?," he ought to have answered, "No, we're not."

With the children grown, the Lindberghs sold the big house in Darien, reserving a portion of the property as a site for a new and much smaller house—the sort of cottage that young people, if they are lucky, move into on getting married. They lived part of the year in Darien, part of the year in a chalet near Vevey, in Switzerland, and part of the year in Maui. Lindbergh's favorite house was the one on Maui. As soon as the doctors in New York told him that he was dying, that was where he wanted to be. Back in the fifties, President Eisenhower had restored his commission in the Army Air Force and had promoted him to Brigadier General. As General Lindbergh, no doubt he could have requested Army assistance in getting him to Maui, but he preferred making his own arrangements; he would fly to Hawaii on an ordinary commercial flight.

On the morning of that last flight, his doctors accompanied him to the door of the hospital, still protesting his departure. Out of a contrary mingling of devotion to Lindbergh and devotion to his profession, one of the doctors burst out, "But you're abandoning science!" Lindbergh shook his head; in the truth as he saw it, and in the words that he spoke, there was more humor than bitterness. "No," he said, "science has abandoned me." At the airport, it was discovered that there had been an unexpected change of personnel in the crew; the flight would be in charge of a pilot who, some years earlier, had served as a stuntman and stand-in for Jimmy Stewart, when

# LINDBERGH ALONE

Stewart was starring as the young Lindbergh in the movie version of <u>The Spirit of St. Louis</u>. It was an eerie coincidence, but Lindbergh said of it only, "I think I know his name."

When he and Anne and their sons, Jon, Land, and Scott, reached Maui, he had a matter of days to live. As always, he busied himself with plans. He knew where he wanted his grave to be dug and he knew exactly how deep and how wide he wanted it to be. Daily, he asked for reports on the state of the digging—the grave was in rock and it took time. He would have the simplest possible coffin made for him out of eucalyptus wood and he would be buried in a plain shirt and khaki trousers. The church service presented a problem. He had never been a churchgoer and the kind of hymns he had heard sung at funerals struck him as hypocritical. Very well; they would work out the problem of the church. He spoke to his other children by telephone. Everything was in order.

He was wearing an oxygen mask when he began to die, and at first he thought that something had gone wrong with the apparatus feeding air into the mask. It was always his first thought to test his equipment; he reached out as if to take off the mask and then Anne saw in his eyes that he knew that it was not the mask.

Once, from a height of two thousand feet, he sighted the rocky little island of St. Gildas—the summer home of the Carrels, where he was about to make his first visit. As he glided down and circled over the main house, the Carrels came out to wave at him. Two horses galloped across a marshy pasture and he could see—but not hear—a black dog bark. He had timed his arrival for the ebb tide, so he would be able to walk across the sea-bottom from the mainland to St. Gildas. He wrote on a slip of paper that he would be back as soon as he could arrange for the care of his plane and for ground transportation along the coast. He tied the slip of paper to a cloth streamer, weighted the streamer with a stone he had brought along for the purpose, and dropped it over the side of the cockpit. It hit the ground a few yards east of the main house, in a small woods.

On the mainland, he had difficulty finding a place to land. After more than an hour's search, he glided down onto an airfield near the city of Dinan, about seventy miles southeast of St. Gildas. It would be close to midnight, with the tide high, by the time he got back to the coast. Moreover, he was unable to communicate with the Carrels, because they had no telephone. He hired a driver and a car and tossed the emergency rubber raft from his plane into the car, along with his luggage. The north coast of Brittany was in total darkness when they drove into the little village opposite St. Gildas. He could see the island glimmering vaguely at sea, under a few pale stars. He unloaded his gear on a concrete ramp running down into the sea and counted out enough francs to pay his driver. There was hardly a sound after the car left: only the soft lapping of sea-water along the ramp. He pumped up the raft, jointed its oars together, stowed his luggage, shoes, and socks, and set out for the island. He felt his toes pressed against the single thickness of rubber. No more than a bubble of air supported him as he rowed. Each dip of the oars left phosphorescence swirling in its wake. Phosphorescent jellyfish floated at different depths around him. He lost all sense of time and space. His modern world had vanished; he felt as if he had rowed backward through a million years.

He made landfall at St. Gildas on a beach of round stones. His feet slipped as he stepped out into the velvety dark. Since the Carrels had had no idea that he would be crossing the water alone at night, no one had waited up to welcome him. He felt utterly alone and exultant. He hung his raft on his shoulder, picked up his luggage, and began feeling his way toward the still-invisible house.

## Photo Credits

P. iii, Underwood & Underwood. P. 4–5, Underwood & Underwood. P. 7t, Air and Space Museum, Smithsonian Institution. P. 7b, Charles A. Lindbergh Papers, Yale University Library. P. 15, Charles A. Lindbergh Papers, Yale University Library (3). P. 23, Charles A. Lindbergh Papers, Yale University Library. P. 26 (inset), Missouri Historical Society. Pp. 26–27, Charles A. Lindbergh Papers, Yale University Library. Pp. 28–29, Missouri Historical Society. P. 31, Wide World Photos. P. 33, Air and Space Museum, Smithsonian Institution. P. 38 (inset), Missouri Historical Society. Pp. 38–39, Minnesota Historical Society. P. 43, Charles A. Lindbergh Papers, Yale University Library. P. 44t, Missouri Historical Society. P. 44b, Minnesota Historical Society. P. 50, Anne Morrow Lindbergh (3). P. 50br, Charles A. Lindbergh Papers, Yale University Library. P. 51, Anne Morrow Lindbergh. P. 58t, Anne Morrow Lindbergh. P. 58b, Charles A. Lindbergh Papers, Yale University Library. P. 59, Charles A. Lindbergh Papers, Yale University Library. P. 60, Minnesota Historical Society (2). P. 67, Minnesota Historical Society (2). P. 72, Charles A. Lindbergh Papers, Yale University Library (2). P. 72br, Anne Morrow Lindbergh. P. 73, Charles A. Lindbergh Papers, Yale University Library (2). P. 84, Minnesota Historical Society (2). P. 85, Minnesota Historical Society. P. 94, Charles A. Lindbergh Papers, Yale University Library. P. 95, Underwood & Underwood. Pp. 98–99, Minnesota Historical Society. P. 104, Minnesota Historical Society. P. 105, Minnesota Historical Society (3). P. 113t, Anne Morrow Lindbergh. P. 113b, Air and Space Museum, Smithsonian Institution. P. 116t, Minnesota Historical Society. P. 116b, Anne Morrow Lindbergh. P. 117t, Charles A. Lindbergh Papers, Yale University Library. P. 117b, Air and Space Museum, Smithsonian Institution. P. 132, Air and Space Museum, Smithsonian Institution (2). P. 133t, Charles A. Lindbergh Papers, Yale University Library. P. 133b, Missouri Historical Society. P. 134t, Charles A. Lindbergh Papers, Yale University Library. P. 134b, Air and Space Museum, Smithsonian Institution. Pp. 148–149, Missouri Historical Society. P. 152t, Wide World Photos. P. 152b, Charles A. Lindbergh Papers, Yale University Library. P. 153t, Underwood & Underwood. P. 153b, Missouri Historical Society (2). P. 164, Missouri Historical Society. Pp. 164–165, Charles A. Lindbergh Papers, Yale University Library. P. 168, Charles A. Lindbergh Papers, Yale University Library (2). P. 168b, Air and Space Museum, Smithsonian Institution. P. 169, Underwood & Underwood. P. 172, Charles A. Lindbergh Papers, Yale University Library (2). P. 173, Missouri Historical Society (2). P. 180, Charles A. Lindbergh Papers, Yale University Library. P. 181, Wide World Photos. P. 183t, Anne Morrow Lindbergh. P. 183b, Air and Space Museum, Smithsonian Institution. Pp. 194–195, Charles A. Lindbergh Papers, Yale University Library (2). P. 200, Charles A. Lindbergh Papers, Yale University Library (2). P. 201t, Joseph D. Ryle. P. 201, Charles A. Lindbergh Papers, Yale University Library (2). Pp. 204–5, Charles A. Lindbergh Papers, Yale University Library. P. 205 (inset), Anne Morrow Lindbergh. P. 215, Charles A. Lindbergh Papers, Yale University Library.

## Acknowledgment

For help in writing this book, I would like to thank my editor, Steven M. L. Aronson, and Russell W. Fridley, John Grierson, Iver Kern, Linda Lee, John T. Rivard, Judith Schiff, and Terry Zaroff.